punk rock or new wave music kept him *really alive* at that time, somehow reflecting or building-in political or social concerns to a level that is sustained by current injustice (or something).

Punkiness was never about proportion, was it? The world still ain't – and won't ever be – good enough. That boy Walton knows and feels this... and still wants some kind of change.

If this sounds bit joyless then na. On the contrary. Your writer's life is full of tremendous, uplifting, wonderful experience – of *poetry*. And gob-smacking people. It's just that anger *is* an energy for him. The Enquiry in here is not so much to forensically reveal the source of some emotive and/or existential rage – this may after all be a profoundly unscientific business – as to dig out some old vinyl and enjoy. And maybe hope that **today** dynamic, engaged rock 'n roll can do its thing all over again.

I0080135

Also by Rick Walton, from Grosvenor House Publishing:

'The Dots Will Not Be Joined'. A generous rampage through a life in sport and coaching. A compendium of ideas.

'Beautiful Games'. How and why we gotta get active. Meaning. Sports Development.

Together I have been known to refer to the three books as my #lolsobiography. Which may be daft, or counter-productive. But if there is mischief, there is also truth – truth some of you will surely recognize.

Read the covers? You want more blurb? It's here...

This is arguably the third part – *so three books* – in Rick Walton's #lolsobiography concerning life, sport, music. But 'Power Chords' will, can and does stand independent of 'The Dots Will Not Be Joined' and 'Beautiful Games'.

The author has always wanted his work to be explainer-lite, but concedes that you newbies may need to know stuff. He is a writer and sports coach. He has over 600 blogs up on't internet, via bowlingatvincent.com (on absolutely everything) and sportslaureate.co.uk, which covers mainly cricket, football and coaching. He has ECB Accreditation for attending cricket, as a 'freelance bloggist'. There are awards on the shelf for contributions to sport. There is a genuinely unique voice in action – 'authentic, wise and beautiful'.

This further incidental autobiography is dedicated to Victor Edward Dodsworth, Nancy-Elizabeth Dodsworth, Keith Winston Walton, Julie Anne Walton and Ken and Marie Roper. And to friends, artists and sportspeople – people who have made the author's life (and all of our lives) rich. It also offers a humble and grateful nod to A & P of Brizzle, who have provided wonderful and sustaining hospitality to a wandering maniac.

*

I remember writing something about seam bowling; how it's tough, tough to be consistent and very tempting to 'change your action', especially (I imagine) when playing at a higher level, where coaches feel they have to suggest something.

I get the need to stay fit (i.e. avoid injury) and always look to progress. But my hunch is that mostly we need to stay true to ourselves. I say to bowlers under my care "it's got to feel like you". And I wonder if maybe we could extend this out, into, yaknow, life itself?

*

This book, perhaps not unusually, is off in search of the things that made its writer. But it's different again, and if there is any arrogance implicit in that quest – by the way, the author does know he's a nobody[1] – it is hoped that genuine and generally-relatable stuff will assuage concerns around sheer egotism.

Themes include the power of ideas and music; particularly when they pour in to teenage life. Identifying with or finding people that speak for you. But early life, too: so of course family and experiences at school, quality of adventure and support, quality of love and environment, mates and comrades. The growth, perhaps, of like-mindedness and the concomitant recognition of things to oppose.

Rick Walton, ultimately sports coach and writer, feels the years 1976-1982/3/4 were monumental in terms of weighing-in to his whole way of being. He knows that

---

[1] ...A-and is entirely at ease with that.

The bowlingatvincent multinational
corporation brings you

POWER CHORDS

BY
RICK WALTON

Grosvenor House
Publishing Limited

This book is published by
Grosvenor House Publishing Ltd
Link House
140 The Broadway, Tolworth, Surrey, KT6 7HT.
www.grosvenorhousepublishing.co.uk

A CIP record for this book
is available from the British Library

Paperback ISBN 978-1-83615-433-4

CONTENTS

#Artist's statement: (the artist is grinning behind the doorway, looking at you, babes).

This is a book about important things in my life, in the hope that some of those things feel or felt important to you.

I should offer the warning that though throughout this escapade I'll be trying *really hard* to be honest and 'make sense', this may not always prove achievable. I foam at the mouth when I go on about certain things, notably sport and music – oh, and probably politics. Or fall back distractedly in the presence of intoxicating blurs half-remembered. So chronological or logical this is not. Clear of error, this is not.

There is no doubt that whilst a decent dollop of what was essential and even universal in these boogtastic wonderstories of mine *will* be captured here, I'll be repeating or tripping over the outcrops of later contradiction and/or material fact. Don't pick holes too much: if the memories or storylines come over all 'Nude Descending a Staircase', forgive me. I'm hoping that writing like this brings us closer to a sort of energetic (and maybe even musical) truth.

Rick.

TAKE A LOOK AT THIS HAND.

Hmm. Life overtakes us. We seem set and then gawd-knows-what interveneth.

*I kinda like that: and many of you will already know or have guessed or feared I'm not the sort to meticulously plan some grid-like way through anything. (We're responding to the universe here; it's **really live**). Sure I have *essential themes* lined-up but things burst in, yes?*

I set out to write the third chunk of stories I know to be true: that's still going to happen. So it's not that this aspiration is going to be entirely de-railed; more that startlingly noteworthy things have and are intervening. Physical things. Hands. Or hand.

Guitars are biggish in this book, because music is MASSIVE in my life. I'm no Jimmy Page but a) choons have really driven me and b) there's one of those weird, meaningless-or-seminal gaps in The Walt Narrative where I maybe should have inserted songwriting and performing. I have and can or could play guitars, passably. At the moment of writing, I can't. Du Pruyten's Contracture. It's been quite a ride.

Du Pruyten's is a thing, it really is, though I'd never heard of it until the doc looked at my ingrowing fingers. Two of them; pinkie and the fella adjacent, on my left hand, gradually but then relentlessly angling in towards the palm. Really quite odd and then really quite concerning for a bloke who makes his living coaching cricket. (Not much fun catching a ball; completely impossible to put on a mitt, for best part of eighteen months). Plus awkward in General Life.

I got tremendously lucky, after my eighteen-month wait to see a consultant. He understood 'this was about my work' as much as the wider muddling through. Meaningful urgency in the picture. He saw – yup – that two fingers needed sorting. Then, in one of the better moments, he told me he could do something about it in about three months – not the two or three years I had feared. (Turns out the local Day Operations Posse can slice me up *in October* – so immediately after the cricket season – and I might be good as new for the spring! Yooo byoootyy!!)

It almost worked out like that. Had the op bang on schedule. (Stunningly brutal cutting into the hand, in a tactical zigzag[2]: plenty stitches). Needed Proper Painkillers, probably for the first time in my life, because hands, being wonderful, are chockfull of nerve-endings and therefore drop emphatically into the Sensitive Metherfekker category of appendages. (No way could

---

[2] Found this quite interesting – hence the note. Apparently a zigzag more efficient than two longish cuts down the line of the tendons(?) or fingers(?) or something. Sounded compelling enough.

I have slept, for the first coupla days, post-op. Not without Cocodamol).

I went back to hospital, as requested, about eleven days after the Stanley-knifing. Hand not looking too bad but still sore-ish and puffy around the wound, with the horror-film stitching still looking deathly black and defiantly un-softened. But you could see the incision was healing; just not what you would call sealed – not entirely.

The nurses thought it looked pretty normal for that stage so teased out the stitches as per the original plan. This was done with real care, for which I was grateful: the web of netting did look a bit like something off a trawler. Going in there I knew there was scope for some notable grief – expertly avoided. I was re-bandaged and the splint that was immediately, post-operatively applied was fixed within the wrapping and plastering.[3] Job done.

Except not. Two days later, I think without any obvious foolish lurches or exertions, the wound opened. It didn't look great. Both kids are lifeguards with goodish first aid training and they both thought a return to hospital was necessary. Taking a ver-ry deep breath – this was Saturday – I went back in.

---

[3] Hmm. Not sure about the timing of some of this – whether I came out from that stitches-removal scene with all the original, post-op fluff, bandaging, splinting and plastering still on board or what. Maybe it doesn't matter. I have no issues what the guys at Withybush Hospital did – even now.

*It took about twenty minutes to get triaged but then five hours to see a doctor. (No real issues. It was what I expected). But because the Day Surgery team were **not in**, because of the weekend, and the doctor was either under some protocol to hand back over to them, or was just stressed and busy, he said I would need to come back on the Monday to see the other guys. This I understood but it also felt unfortunate, at the very least, as the wound was visibly open and one side of the incision had kinda separated and sprung up and apart – not wildly, but clearly – from the other 'flap'. Plus a good mate of ours (also a doctor) had been sent pics of the hand by my kids: he responded by saying either re-stitch or stick some butterfly stitches in there. I used my world-level diplomacy skills to ask the hospital doc *incredibly politely and unthreateningly* whether butterfly stitches might be an option. He stumbled a little but stuck to his plan, before giving me more anti-biotics and moving on.*

I still have no significant issues with this. On the contrary I will note to the universe that over the period of my free care at Withybush Hospital, Haverfordwest, I was overwhelmingly well-treated and looked after by individuals from all over the world. They were largely courteous, professional and kind. I may have been unfortunate to unavoidably land with them on a weekend for that final visit. *Maybe* the stitches could have stayed in for another few days. Whatever; things went a bit pear-shaped.

I knew that by the time Monday came around the plasters applied across the wound to flatten-out and re-align that part which had lifted would have done enough to hold things together. There had been an obvious setback but there would be enough of an improvement, if I took care, for the thing to heal – just bit slower and later than was ideal. In short there was not much point in going back in (for another long wait) and for the nurse/doc to say 'well yes, we can see there's been a problem there but it looks like it's starting to heal again'. So I didn't go. Because it had started back on that road.

I looked after my hand; kept it clean and covered and barely moved it. I think I did use some simple antiseptic cream and I did take some homeopathy[4] and over days then weeks the wound healed really well. So what's the problem?

*Truth is I can't be sure. But whilst the primary aspiration to straighten out the fingers has been 90% successful, movement of three fingers **back in**, towards the palm, has been damaged. I can't (currently about five months after surgery) get anywhere near making a closed fist with my left hand. This despite ongoing (bloody painful) but skillfully executed physio from the treble-fabulous Lorna. The knuckle-joints in the affected fingers are more-or-less seized. The top of my little finger is stiff as wood and the fella next to it is not great. Even the middle finger, which was never operated-upon, is cranky and unhelpful, particularly at the last joint.*

---

[4] Know plenty of folks think this a nonsense but hey-ho – different strokes. I'm open-minded on that.

Lorna and myself are both massaging, manipulating and stretching all four fingers. It's been wintry so I go in to physio – fortnightly, originally and now weekly – wearing shedloads of clobber to try and keep the hand warm, and therefore hopefully malleable, pre-action. We laugh a little that I have to peel off as soon as I get in, because we both know I will be sweating like hell – even under the eyes – when those thin blue surgical gloves start stroking then bending digits three, four and five.

The pain is almost fascinating but it hurts too much for the experience to stay entirely scientific – unless doing yoga breaths to keep the grief at bay counts as science? I do dread the sessions on one level but am also grateful for the time and effort going in. Thus far it's only reasonable to report that there has been almost no progress. (We actually have a crunch session tomorrow – Wednesday 11th March 2025 – when we may decide if Lorna jacks on this). Again I would have no complaints. Something outside of our control has happened: we've tried about as hard as anyone could to retrieve the situation.

But why all this wittering about MY HAND, fer chrissakes?!?

*Because this book is about the **power of music**; in my life and beyond. And it's personal; about things I know or have done or experienced, including (hah!) buying **and playing guitars**. As it stands I am now nowhere near being able to do that again – believe me, I've tried. This is the intrusion into my life and this book. It's rich and it feels BIG.*

PROLOGUE.

Where to start, in terms of family life and culture? Or maybe specifically music? And how to know when awarenesses became so developed, or grief, shock or hormones took over so completely that the whole of my life became about defiance. Because I think maybe it did. And this feeds in to everything.

But maybe before the ideas-fest and the tribal allegiances kick-in we need to go eyeball to eyeball. And do that thing where we try to accommodate. I have strong opinions on some things which may have arisen from my love of music. (This book is about that process – or speculations about how mere choons can shape or contribute to a life). It feels extraordinary and kinda thrilling to me that anything so flimsy and unbodied could be so fabulous and enormous. I'm really hoping you have some personal sense or experience of that.

Where we need to accommodate is in the sphere of politics and philosophy. It would be raw dumb of me to alienate readers who don't share or who actively resent my direction of travel. But it's going to happen. What I would ask is that all-comers respect the energy and love in this bundle. They are both true. I absolutely believe in the daft and angry things you're going to hear and I hope you can accept them with a grace that maybe

I don't deserve... unless you factor in the love of music and the faith, therefore, in things which can inspire and convert us. If nothing else, this book is a tribute to the creative and *that which moves us*. Much more than it's a polemic – I hope.

Anyway, where were we? Oh yeh: here goes. Defy the shock of people dying. Then before you know it defy the evil that was Thatcher[5]. Wade in there. Defy the bigotry and prejudice criminally at large and *in some way* oppose the privilege. All this in a teen rage. Then *live up to* those who came before, whilst knowing they were different – maybe simpler, better – and that things don't or can't work like that. But let them still be your gods.

Don't fer Christ's sake out yourself as such – faaar too pretentious, far too self-righteous! – but absolutely *be* a protest singer. Be the inevitable mad mixture that you feel; of hard, deep thinker and honest force. Be immune to judgements from outside; be fearless and pour the good energy in. Time will or may come when you can be more *accepting*. For now, trust and work and be conscious. These things have value.

*

The moment is everything: accident-of-birth catapulting me simultaneously into a hormone-fest *and* Anarchy in the UK meant this particular youth was inevitably a Child of That Time. Driven or pumped. Scarred, maybe.

---

[5] Should I have added 'in your view?' Stay with me and forgive?

Furious, definitely; judgmental definitely. Carrying a load, probably.[6] Deeply lost but as deeply certain as most teens – yes? – that he would do things in enflamed opposition to the pitiful acquiescence that was Normal Life. So yeh, off-the-scale indulgent in some respects but also having a kind of rebellious integrity.

People died on us and I'm not going to tell their stories here. There's enough of that in the previous books. You just need to register the possibility that maybe everything Yours F Truly does is a kind of amorphous, inadequate, good-natured but politicised homage to three great 'ordinary' blokes. This is not to say that I am a hugely party-political animal, or that I under-appreciate the Walton Women: but it rightly implies that I'm on a permanent slow-burn around how the world just ain't good enough, in a way that those better men simply weren't.

There's generational stuff in play here, because a) life *was* simpler and b) in some senses it was less aware. Folks just didn't know or couldn't know the world, its peoples and its foibles in the way we can now. (Not that this makes us any more educated). Plus sentiment. I may gush, or goddammit not be able to see[7], or drown us in the kind of emotive slippage we're all prone to. This is what love does: this is what age does.

---

[6] Went to see some weirdo, many years later, after a heart episode. He looked at me and immediately asked why I was carrying the world's troubles. 'I'm seeing a yolk across your shoulders'.

[7] Yup. Definitely prone to welling-up.

I may never know if these old guys were *just wiser*, apparently swerving the day-to-day cataclysms that eat away at me/you/us, but however dubiously old-school it may sound, here's my daft Braveheart moment: *raises fist*.

I am proud to be of them. Always, I will love, revere and follow them, or try to, for their invincible (yes) and endless (yes it was!) honesty and humility. They are recalled in the hope that we can all, in the modern idiom, stand on their elephantine shoulders.

*

I guess the thing that stirs me the most is the urgent need to change the universe. And that **really may be a** direct result of **punk** and Margaret Thatcher.

Bit loathe to put dates into this baby but it may be inescapable. Absolutely not telling you freeloaders my birth date – not until we're mates and you've proved you're worth it – but suppose I can offer the rough figuration that I was a furious and pyrotechnically hormonal late-teen when the over-combed one began to preen through and over our lives. She, and Rotten's voice, and Strummer's heart, and Costello's lyrics and my father's death were the things that made me. They were contingent and co-forming energies that powered and power me towards trying, at the very least, to live a life that *opposes*.

This book, the third part (so far) in my #lolsobiography, is inevitably about that. But it's also about sport, about influence, about how wonderful things are, even when darkness and dumbness and the twisted evils of money and privilege continue to pin us to the deck. My faith in art and music and sport never dims. My faith in the Three Great Mates we all have and need and my two sensational kids carries me through.

*

Life seems to have conspired towards poles of opinion, not just on social media but that might be the most obvious example. Too many of us make judgements that are ill thought-out or unforgiving. We're bawling our truths at each other. We exercise (or exorcise?) a kind of manic certainty that draws us into conflict rather than conversation. Everything from the Twitters[8] to PMQs contributes to this.

Let me put on record my own weakness in this regard: I get angry and I judge. But in my heart I know that tolerance – and knowing that you may be wrong – are amongst the most essential of human virtues. We do have to judge; we do have to decide; we do need to get better but we also need to be civil. That's not a recipe for capitulation.

Takes further deep breath. Look I'm as ready as the next bloke to launch into *Grandstanding Mode*. The Times and the Socials and everything about now make *GM* the engaged individual's 'natural' response, do they

---

[8] Yeh I know, now X. Pipe down!!

not? Us punters are being teased towards some angry vortex all the time. Ah: cue some polar expeditionism.

We live, it strikes me, in an extraordinary and dangerous moment. The West is arguably madder than it's ever been, with the Trump/Musk coalition-thing a catastrophic threat to the intelligence, knowledge and goodness that underpins society itself. (It's November 2024 as I write: we await the second Trump term but Brother Elon has sculpted the matrix into an angry monster). The truth has suffered an especially foul Special Op'[9] – Bannon's infamous shitstorm. Those previously relatively harmless *Influencers* (think makeovers, think pranksters, posers and dancers) have morphed into combat-ready sub-nazis.

This is a challenge. It can drag us down and have us raging at (and waaay beyond) the deliberately-reduced politics we now suffer in the West.

So don't expect me to qualify everything – I may fall short! I know we're well-advised to avoid cheap blame-games but I'm still gonna launch, here and there. Of course under-privileged and under-educated people have always been likely to 'strike out'. Of course this general discontent has always been weaponized by people with hands on the levers. But there are lines we just don't cross; there are things which are just plain wrong.

---

[9] Deliberate perversion of things we thought were fixed and factual. Facilitated by socials/moguls/what we might call the Extremist Establishment.

The Great Families and the oligarchs; the MAGA cult and the 'gammon'; the liars and the cheats and the racists *are **bad folks**.*[10] Some more, some less. We who feel this may be entitled to tell them that, although this is likely to be inflammatory. 'We see you'. But we also have to deal with them – by that, I mean debate, include, educate – however difficult or unlikely that may seem. And, perhaps before we inter-react, or rise to condemn, or commit the sin of prejudice ourselves, we have to go big and go public on the idea that they, these people, are as valuable as we are. They have our right to argue.

It may not get much tougher than to accept that the 'racist morons' or 'easily-led' on our streets or in our timelines are *people we have to appreciate* but... we do. Whilst opposing them.

Where lies progress in all this? On a political level I suppose we need to elect governments that will be a) strong enough morally to oppose prejudice and b) smart enough economically to improve the lot of the disaffected. Clearly, sadly, the momentum appears to be going the other way in certain key democracies.

This brings us back into the circle of action, or exasperation. There is a kind of backstop, a point of no further retreat for many of us. Prejudice and privilege are wrong. Whether entitled or powerless, ignorant or driven, player or played, they are wrong. We can and should choose to do better around those things – we surely *have to?* This implies all kinds of stuff but let's

---

[10] Read on before you judge...

just call it goodness. Most of us recognize it, even if we choose not to 'walk in its path'. There are a million distractions, some gorgeous, some filthy. We need to be decent and fair and friendly; to find the invincibly *moral* core. That can be common; can define us.

But hang on. In the face of Trumpism and Reform, alt-rightism and this *galaxy of loss,* what's our civil/intellectual/physical/cultural *reaction?* Depends who we are. Are we leaders or passengers or artists or victims? Who do we look to, where do we go? Weirdly, it seems a scientific certainty that there will be a response, even in this turbulent evil. (Is that not how the universe works?) The response may even be a thing of glory and inspiration.

Wonderfully, we make our statements in a myriad of ways. As the mighty Slits did, we can *'create'*; kick up a fuss; make something challenging and radical and beautiful. We may need to do more, but this is part of the change – or at least one irrepressibly human, principal means to strike back. Let's *create*. Let's be anti-badness; anti-racist; anti- any declining status quo. Our pens *are* 'snug as a gun'.[11] Our fingers *are* on the fretboard. This is part of life's purpose.

---

[11] Slits: 'Typical Girls', from 'Cut'. Seamus Heaney: 'Digging'.

ONE – YEAR DOT.

I was born at number 30-something Southwold Crescent, Grimsby; the third son of four. (No blue plaque yet). Both parents were teachers. I think we were probably pretty skint in those early years; certainly our dad worked in factories or similar during school holidays to find an extra bob or two. You could do that then.

At least one of my bro's was born in the nursing home on the Nunsthorpe Estate, which wasn't then known for its leafy opulence. We could use this (and similar) to tick the street credibility box but given the privileges we all increasingly leaned into (or earned) over time, that would be conspicuously fraudulent. Southwold Crescent was base-camp for a while but I believe a colleague from dad's school also pointed us to a flat somewhere else in town: this is unconfirmed and you may be bored of the Humble Beginnings vibe already, anyhow. (HB? It *was* and then it wasn't, coz of intelligence and hard work – however gruesomely neoliberal that might sound).

This *is here*, this crushingly unnecessary detail, about patently insignificant people, because we cannot exclude the possibility that geographic/sociological minutiae do indeed play some sort of meaningful wider role in development. (They *must do*, surely?) Even in the case of non-Influencers like us. Plus there are better stories upcoming.

There is evidence, in the form of a fabulous and poignant postcard sent by my now long-dead father to his later completely blind Auntie Annie, that indicates a stint above the cobblers, in Station Road, Healing. This, from 1958, before I was born, both represented a significant upgrade and a sign that our parents were right on the case in terms of sorting the loveliest environment they could reach to bring up the young fam. The cobblers is sadly also long-gone.

(One of the lovely things about writing about families is the gems that turn up. Ask your folks a question and)...

I've only just seen the postcard. Given the shocking nature of dad's death – cardiac arrest, aged 44 – it got the heartstrings a-twinkling.

Auntie Annie was one of the few remaining relatives from the previous generation still in his hometown of Macclesfield. (Both of dad's parents died before he was 18). When we visited, years later, Annie's eyesight was completely gone. She *did do* that flutter-of-the-hands across our faces, to feel for our Waltonian features. It was strange, alright, but not exactly scary. I think I remember her smiling as she mapped us with her ancient fingertips. And that strong Macc accent. Reaching back 55 years and probably more, what registers is a moment where a really old lady was really friendly. And that made it okay: okay then and wonderful now.

Auntie Annie died at 99. (Cruel, huh?) Don't know why but the line in dad's card that reads 'My radishes have grown a foot!' made me beam... then brought the tears close. Something to do with that daft pride. Something to do with different times.

*

Mother's recall is a bit sketchy around all of this. There may have been just the two Walton Boys in Healing, first time around. (So 1958-9?) Then Southwold Crescent and the arrival of Richard James, shortly before we flit to Hong Kong, when I was ten months old. (Epic story, if anything underplayed: some portion of it recounted in 'Beautiful Games'). Hard to reconcile the quietish, relatively undemonstrative nature of our parents with the wild gambles they took us into – two, then three, then four tiny lads.

I think mum (on her own!) took three lads *under four years of age* on three different planes to get to HK. She'd never been abroad; Dad was already there, 'sorting accommodation'. Apparently complete strangers 'just mucked-in and helped her' on the flights. The notion of 't'other end of the world' barely applies, these days. Feck me, it did in 1961.

*

A fair characterization of this period – first half of the 60's, either side of and including our Hong Kong adventure[12] – would be 'Young, Expanding Family

---

[12] See 'Beautiful Games!'

Works Like Hell, To Get Somewhere'. Mum's parents were local so no doubt bailed us out in a million ways but there was no money in the family background, despite the fact her father, our 'grandpa', played football at one time for the sporting behemoth that is Manchester United. (Holy shit! Imagine if we had that wedge in the family now!)[13]

Look I'm probably perversely proud of my home town but let's get past the name, the jokes, the film(s) and the imagery. Yes there were dodgy flats and drunken fishermen. Yes parts of it were and are 'tough'. But there are areas of Grimsby that are genuinely pleasing on the eye and that ole chestnut about solid, friendly Northern Folk absolutely holds true, for me. (Oh and we **are** of the North: don't you dare call us Midlanders or East Midlanders! No offence, George Dobell).

My strong impression is that our particular branch of the Walton family, like the rest of 'em in my experience, was powered by lots of love and hard graft. And even a relative anti-capitalist like myself appreciates working *towards something* – what we now call 'mobility' – can be good. We got out of town early. Our parents were smart to the blessings that fields and relative quiet can offer. Meaning us kids grew up not in some 'bruising estate' but almost next door to a bloody big sports field:

---

[13] Whilst we're talking money and status, I should confirm that we did, as a mob, become upwardly mobile – because of that aforementioned hard graft. We bought a semi-detached in Healing for £2,000 in about 1965. That *was* leafy – and therefore significantly privileged.

Healing British Legion. And what a gift to our lives that was.

It's barely an exaggeration to say that for the decade 1964-74, *after* the three years in Honkers, which are cruelly almost completely beyond my recall, we lived in a wonderful, energetic daze. Just in North Lincs, as opposed to the New Territories, China.

Mostly football, the whole dreamy lump of it. Football and *playing*. Kick-ball-fly. Jumping wildly into the dyke at the back of the Legion, onto and into a child-infested cushion of hay, sending those half-buried or half-awake scampering to the bank, to launch themselves again, possibly from some alarmingly flimsy tree, almost certainly screaming "Gerronniiimmo-ooo!!" Building straw dens out of bales. Running or doing that fast walk thing that kids do, on our way to our mates, or the 'Leej'[14] or the park. And yes we did climb Big Trees and camp-out in gardens and build obstacle-courses: hah, we *timed ourselves* racing round them! And if this sounds boyish and innocent and bloody healthy then that's because it was.

Ok. A moment's grown-up reflection may be called-for.

Understand if there are now concerns about a) that word, *boyish* and/or b) the muscularity/'competitiveness' of what we did. Accept both conflict with modern understandings, which I respect. Neither looking to offend contemporary sensibilities nor use descriptors in

---

[14] British Legion. (Field).

a hostile or unknowing way. Factoid: I never read them but there were probably still 'Boy's Own' magazines when I was a nipper, which is almost funny but also kinda terrifying. It wasn't just us kids who knew nothing about gender, the whole world was void of these issues: which is to say it was as ignorant as it was innocent.[15]

At the time I am describing it's fair to say we were pretty damn boyish. Now we would frame all of these experiences differently, quite rightly. I know, dear friends that gender and identity is rather appallingly one of the great battle-grounds of our age. Feels like whatever any of us says can be weaponized. Broadly though, the possibility to express your humanity in the way most appropriate for yourself is a pretty fabulous aspiration, surely? So despite offering clunky 'own goals' aplenty around this, that's what I hold onto: the idea that the old binaries are too simplified, too ungenerous. But hey; I am straight and middle-aged and deeply, deeply flawed. Let's move swiftly on to stuff I know about.

*

There was school, I suppose and so o-kaaay there were other formative experiences, outside of or beyond the relentless footie-fest. The village primary was presided-over by a psychotic Scotsman who stood at the hall door so that every single child had to say "excuse me, sir" as they filed in for assembly. If they didn't, he had a

---

[15] Possible, I suppose that someone may howl that this is a travesty. I accept it's a *generality*.

word. I was a decent kid and good at the learning malarkey so rarely had dealings. But this was plainly powerfully odd behaviour. He was a sort of quietish megalomaniac, who bought a shiny new suit for each school concert. It was the garb of a zealot and, annually updating, he conducted petrified generations of kids through 'Supercalifragilisticexpiallidocious' with a particular charm that was as close to wild misapplication as it was to leadership.

Mr Russell rarely interacted with us, outside of rehearsals for, then execution of, the concert. He turned into a different bloke, on the day – not without a certain sparkle. He 'conducted'. It was a kind of mischievous capture: we didn't know what the phrase 'being held hostage' meant, back in 1967, but this might have been it. Mrs Whitley and Mrs Watson, on the other hand, were off-the-scale fabulous. Generous; friendly; loving in exactly the way that an Early Years teacher should be. For clarity (and fairness) should confess that the former is my best mate's mum. She remains an absolute goddess, beyond 90.

I was recently given a class pic from Healing County Primary School which tugged heavily and made me realise how BIG those times and connections were. In my case they really were largely idyllic. Coz Stevie Blendell, Wayne Okopskyj, Mark Moss, Linda Dye and Helen Sitch and the rest were bloody wonderful. I could feel and smell and hear them, in that picture. Made me remember football and school sports on the playing-field; skating or 'sliding' on the playground in proper snow and ice; getting 8 out of 5 for something I wrote (about Guy Fawkes, I think). And even the dinners, which I loved. Stodgy, honest food that I've not entirely left behind. Maybe the meat was thin and the mash lukewarm after that queueing... but Eve's pudding and custard! Or some kind of jam sponge! Bloo-dee Nora.

True, semolina and rose-hip syrup was more of a challenge. And the day that the milky-smooth semolina turned into a full-on frogspawn was a riot. But though I'm already considering deleting that word 'honest'... and I know those gert big lumps of carbs and sugars weren't great... I *did* enjoy stuffing school dinners into my weedy frame: for better or worse. Food was about comfort and volume. It still kinda is. And I still don't really go out to eat because it feels like some weird extravagance.

There were 'incidents' no doubt but my Primary School experiences do kinda coalesce into a very innocent loveliness. Why wouldn't they?

Mr Ord's football boots: he was about sixty at the time, so *absolutely ancient*, but the footwear looked older – like something out of Van Gogh. *Games*, inside and outside of lessons. The day that I threw a medium-light, so harmlessly-shrivelled conker at nobody – just threw it, exuberantly – and it hit one of the strikingly beautiful Appleton girls, standing about four miles away at the other end of the playground, an inch below her left eye. Mr Ord, largely an even-tempered man, gave us all an intense dressing-down and demanded that the culprit identified himself: I was too damn scared.

Phillip Butler had a season ticket to stand outside Mr Russell's office. Helen Sitch and Linda Dye both drank salt water in a pact to avoid school. Half the village knew about it but (I think because they were both generally good sorts) the repercussions were not major: our Scotch über-lieutenant being eminently capable of delivering brazenly partial justice.

One day 'Jock' Russell was leaning over me whilst I worked at my desk. I remember it ver-ry clearly. There was something palpably intimidating about this, maybe because of the length of time he breached my personal space for *and* the unnerving proximity. He *did have* a presence and he knew it. I have an acute memory that the longer he stayed over me,[16] the closer I got to elbowing the fekker good and hard, in the solar plexus. But I didn't – fortunately. On very rare occasions I think all of Messrs Russell, Ord and Wood did break out the slipper or the ruler-over-the-knuckles. Mostly though, the catchment being a gift, they could exercise authority at a civilized level.

Primary School was mostly wonderful. There was learning and there was love.

---

[16] Not making any hugely significant allegations, here. It was just strangely disconcerting. And it could only have been him.

TWO – SECONDARY MODERN.

I was medium-brainy. Throughout school this meant there was a real, active imperative towards affecting sufficient male normalcy so as to avoid getting battered or exposed as a puff.[17] (I mean this. Being clever, especially when being built like a weed, was a proper threat to your life, or certainly the quality of your life, which *had to be laddish*). Fortunately I was sporty and could make folks laugh.

At Secondary School I was neither a teacher's pet nor driven to achieve, but I did okay. Not entirely clear if I attended Grammar School for just the one year, before it switched to comprehensive status – think this is correct – but it feels like I managed that medium-seismic shift reasonably well. You 'just do', as a young 'un, yes? (Or maybe not?!?)

Clee Grammar School for Boys may sound bit posh, but it wasn't. It was just the state school that lads from the area went to, if they had happened to pass the eleven plus. I can't remember anything *at all* about that exam process, but I did pass it and was therefore bound to jump on the bus into Cleethorpes every morning, a

---

[17] Read Beautiful Games.

trip of about forty minutes from semi-rural Healing. It was a pret-ty healthy fifteen minutes yomp to the bus stop at the top of the village; possibly more. So a brilliant and what we might today regard as facilitating way to start the educational day. We did march up there nearly every morning.

The *bus journeys* really were a part of our lives that now seems estranged: not because we're too posh for public transport but because for three of us Walton Lads growed-up, rural or semi-rural life means we suck heavily at the nipple of the internal combustion engine – regrettably. It may say something sociologically interesting or even uncomplimentary about our lives that none of us find ourselves on buses anymore. That registers with me now as something of a loss. Eldest bro' lives in London, using tube and overground mainly: when I visit I like to jump on the bus but the Speed and Convenience Imperative often mitigates against.

Mid to late-stage school career, a particular mate would bring a portable cassette-player to the top deck and infuriate the majority of the population by booming-out Slaughter and the Dogs. Every morning at about 8 am – so major-league brass, fair play. I remember polite-but-hostile looks but not sure if anybody *actually asked him* to turn the bloody thing off. Maybe once. There were capable young people on that bus; fifty youths of between about eleven and eighteen, boys and girls. Pick-ups from Immingham, Stallingborough and Healing; all of them apparently too nice to intervene. 'M', king of immovable insensitivity in those days, is now rather magnificently Head of Psychology at a Northern University.

Fairly sure Clee Grammar is now a nursing home. Back then it was a manageable-sized and relatively supportive establishment which offered those ubiquitous but wildly different contemporary experiences: namely growing up; making lifelong mates; doing lots of sport; learning a token amount of *Latin(!)* and dodging the fucking hooligans from rival schools, who would occasionally march past and pick on someone.

This was the time – into the '70s – when life felt a bit over-run with football hooligans. It was scary, or I found it so. Can recall vividly one particular occasion when a group of complete tossers from the rival Secondary School slunk past. We were fearful of them and they knew it; they loved it. Being on the main road, out the front of the school seemed like it should offer some protection; but na. One of them, inevitably equipped with closely-cropped barnet and DM boots, kicked one of our lot *really hard*, up on his thigh, as he was tramping through.

They were singing or taunting or celebrating before and during this shockingly mindless episode. I guess they thought it was a moment of triumph, given that Their Bloke had kicked the biggest lad on our side: twats. The recipient, whom I knew well, could quite possibly have battered the assailant one-to-one, but he turned away and the Lindsey tough-guys moved on. Somebody amongst us asked our lad why he didn't 'have a go back' at the DM-ed moron. To which the reply was something like 'what... and all of us get smashed?'

One year later things had changed somewhat. We were now in Matthew Humberstone Comprehensive School, a monstrously big and initially discomfiting place that I actually kinda came to love. We mixed, extraordinarily quickly and easily, looking back, with a whole lot of well 'ard or delightfully soft boys and girls, the majority of whom had of course failed that previously dangerously-defining test. This was largely pre-hormone onslaught, but there was something thrilling (as well as intimidating) about being close to fledgling or (wow. Jeesus!) fully-formed breasts.

We were 'streamed', certainly, but only in lessons themselves. When we reported in to class first thing or after dinner-break we were amongst the heaving masses – again I came to love this and still view it as being wonderful, valuable, and one of the Things That Made Me. Genuinely. Girls were still an utterly alien species and remained that way for years but I smile now, thinking of how lovely many of them were; even when I was lost and hopeless in their company.

For clarity, brief further memory on this. At Clee Grammar there were *no girls* – they went to *the other* Clee Grammar. This certainly set back the (ahem) social skills of many of us significantly. We weren't destined to be swots and virgins forever but yeh, the vibe was different. Half the world suddenly had talcum powder in its bag. A couple of these girls, *aged twelve*, were like, yaknow, Proper Women.

I know I wasn't an entirely model student but the unhelpfully contradictory fact that I came top of the class in that initial, grammar school year – partly by virtue of coming first in Latin and music – was something I really needed to play down, going forward. I had to get in the footie and cricket teams, be a wag, and generally work hard to cast off any suspicions of wankerdom or worse. I did that stuff.

We had gone from being marked (in end of year exams) in the three or four classes of Clee Grammar, to swimming in the wilder, less regulated stream that was Matthew Humberstone: I think towards a dozen classes per year group. There was less or possibly no old-school testing – no issue with that – and you really were conscious of richness and diversity, brilliance and dumbness. There were 1800 of us, on two sites. There were gaps between lessons so that you could leggit from maths to art. It was definitely edgier.

I suppose we had grown out of bustling round to our mate's house to *play*, by this time but relationships were still largely fixed to sport. My best mates were in the football and cricket team[18] and wow, a zillion years later it's still true that being in a changing-room or on a pitch is about as good as being me gets. The geography has changed – Grimsby/Cleethorpes/North Lincs to West Wales – but not the animating joy of playing team sport. I am entirely at ease with the fact that everything I've ever written re-hashes this ridicu-truism.

---

[18] Inevitably cricket disappeared once we got to Comprehensive School – Matthew Humberstone. No money, no strip.

A decent lump of what passes for my socio-intellectual life may be outside of daft games – I do read, I do walk and I do have a weirdly eccentric weakness for art and art theory – but it's always been the case that sport (or activity) has provided most pleasure, at least *by volume*. (Kids and family aside). Apart from going out on the razz with teenage comrades, have never had a group of friends to do either the 'regular social drink' or dinner-party thing with. Never needed it or had the time or head-space. Sport provided all that stuff.[19]

At school I got in first teams and regional teams and met and played alongside some great guys. Sounds rilly pompous but I do view my comprehensive education generally, and the new team-mates phenomenon specifically, as being central to what I hope is a decent capacity to respect and value people from all corners. Finding that Loser Z in maths and physics is a god of big-hearted brilliance on the footie pitch and Scruffbag Y is a total legend for his wit in the dressing room has been *life-changingly MAJOR*. Things become simple when you know that we all have wonderful stories and we all *must be valued*. Privilege becomes unthinkable – becomes something we have to call the fuck out.

*

I'm a bit concerned that my memory is crap. This is one reason I don't propose to dwell too much on 1970-75.

---

[19] Hasten to add that I pretty much stopped playing sport to play a proper part (I hope) in bringing up our kids. During that period – almost twenty years? – it was my privilege to pour my energy into work/provision/family life. As you do.

Another is that I was just another insect in the crazy swarm at Matthew Humberstone. I did kinda love it but I was swattable and inadequate and just bit mindlessly looking for somewhere to alight. I got through and then suddenly – the sixth form.

We could wear things. There were certainly rules – jackets and trousers, I think, shirts and even ties – but there was a level of 'freedom'. We were, most of us, both self-conscious and not. I had no real interest in which jacket or keks. I may have wanted badges on a denim jacket to go to the village youth club but this was about as far as my interest in sartorial signaling went. In *our* ether, there was about 13% of the current level of peer pressure around fashion and appearance, even I think amongst the girls. Plus for most of us there was definitely a 'family budget' within which we had to operate.

I finished up with a green corduroy jacket. Have no memory of choosing it but must have had some say in that. Can't remember which shop – British Home Stores? C and A? – or which rack, or any sense of satisfaction or meaningful interest around said purchase. It was just shopping... and therefore bollocks.

Day One and Chris Leeming wore a Bobby Dazzler of a checked jacket. He was both proud and almost embarrassed about it. His early concession that it was 'bit on the noisy side' was typically good-natured and appeased any potential sparring. If I remember rightly he had troos to match and unleashed those baybees a day or two later. The whole effect was spectacular in a Piet Mondrian-on-acid kindofaway. Off-white with blue and red check; maybe even some green in there. Proper Do Not Adjust Your Set job. Hell we laughed. But thirty seconds later it was all forgotten; he returned to being Krid, the top, top lad that he was, cut gloriously free from any infringement.

Weeks later – so still in the early stages of our time in the Lower Sixth – I do have a clear memory of going into school wearing dark blue corduroy keks *and* that green jacket. I remember thinking it was a howler before I left home but alternatives were few or nil. Less offensive combo's were either mucky, wet, or "in your dreams, son" so I had to go there. There may have been coupla comments, upon arrival; nothing too cutting, probably just that ubiquitous "oof!" and a raised eyebrow or twelve. But mostly we lads *did think* this clothes stuff was bollocks: guessing this is not quite the same for the Insta/Tik-tok generation?

*

Some of our mates had left, after the fifth year. Notably Col Humphries and Steve Bramley, who like others 'had to go find work'. That was a real blow to the craic and the football team but we understood: it figured. I may have already begun to resent the whole treadmill-into-uni cowabunga, so, with atypical maturity on reflection, respected their *alternative pathways*. A shift had occurred, though; school life had turned, like some heaving supertanker. The next port-of-call – at a distance; abstracted – was to feature just three subjects of study... and girls.

*

I was always going to do English: I was 'good at it' and the lead tutor, John Wilson, was a magbloodynificent fella. Tall, relatively posh but genuinely sympathetic and with a tremendous, sarcastic wit. He pointed us to the Moderns paper, figuring quite rightly that this might be the closest Classic Literature gets to offering half a dozen restless teens from Grimsby/Cleethorpes something approaching relevance. (I/we never did Chaucer or any of that harder-to-reach stuff).

'Doing' Forster and Lawrence and Fitzgerald and Orwell with Mr Wilson was subtly and maybe seminally powerful. For the sheer pleasure of it; for the laughs and camaraderie we shared; and for the brilliance and import of those writers. Hard to quantify in any sense the effect of even the most obviously compelling and beautiful books. Easy to size-up the teacher, John Wilson. He was a great and engaging man.

*

Writing had always been the basis for a certain level of success. (Anybody who can express themselves on the page with any facility has a ludicrous advantage in education, yes?) I came top in Latin and music because I could spell and *pen* stuff. It was complete cobblers but my way in to a sort of elite – the Kids Who Can Write. (In music we had done almost no music, but learned a bit about coupla blokes called Grieg and Beethoven. I splatted out the essays and job done).

I also did Geography – because it was fabulous and the teachers were great – and ultimately Geology. (The Plan had been to do French but I couldn't in the end face the thought of being in a group of *three*, under a particular teacher. It was stupid, plainly, not least because we would probably all have stormed to good grades in a class of that size, but *attitudes* had kicked-in. Plus that Geog/Geol combo would then make a certain sense. I had no idea what I might do, mind, beyond school, other than bring down the established order).

Whoa. This reminds me… so I need to reel back. 'O' Levels; or GCSEs. On reflection – and I find this interesting, even if you, sagacious reader, do not – this *measurement of things* had already begun to stir me up.

It now strikes me as significant *because completely clear*: I was angry about The Crushing Treadmill *before* we took our 'O' Levels. (This is important because it's two or three years before my father died and **before punk took a hold of the universe**). Why am I suddenly so positive that I was raging at this early date? Because, hilarious-but-true, I remember feeling really insulted by the realization that all we had to do to go flying through our exams was re-read some notes and parrot the fekkers. Regurgitate. Not think; not use our intelligence; just remember and simply re-produce. That made me sick.

Set aside momentarily the laughable pomposity in play here, the appalling arrogance of a fifteen/sixteen(?) year-old state school idiot. Just log the fact – for I am hilariously sure of this – that muggins here felt personally affronted by the notion that these exams were a kind of affirmation of dullness and a suffocating repression of individual, imaginative thought. Wow. This figured: it fitted in with the way life was already shaping up. Things *really were* geared towards cogs in the machine. They *really did* want you to mindlessly fall in.

As I write this spleeny-but-embarrassing nonsense now, I promise you I am more aware than I have been for a long, long time, that this *is* what I was feeling, in 1975(?) So I think I already knew that The System was shite... and that I would not and could not, in the soon come words of The Clash, be 'Working for the Clampdown'.

I may need to walk away, make a cuppa tea and consider some more how I got to this place *before* John Lydon and Joe Strummer got to me. Before I do that let me confirm that in both my 'O' and 'A' levels I opted for wild, interesting and challenging questions on some occasions,[20] because a) I really didn't give a fuck about how This System would judge me and b) that just felt more entertaining.

Makes brew...

*

Ok. Factoids gathering or straightening – well, hardly! – as I wait for the metaphorical Earl Grey to cool.

---

[20] Clear memory of NOT doing a geography question on anti-cyclones, coz it SO OBVIOUSLY wanted you to regurgitate notes; was *embarrassingly* easy. Also – quite damagingly I think – I did a question 'for Caribbean Candidates only' in one paper. Should probs have got an A, for Geog 'A' Level. Lols. Got a D!

Dad died whilst I was in the Lower Sixth – so pre- 'A' Levels. That naturally facilitated some of the anger and resentment at the universe. But *it was there before.* And it strikes me that this book will be more than I ever imagined about teasing out where that came from. (So bugger: therapy. I can only apologise!) Political awarenesses were probably creeping in. Those crippling and revelatory and wonderful hormones were storming and waning. The image I have of a relatively-well-rooted teen with great people around him stands firm... but with what, exactly, making this more complicated? Too many ideas? Too much sensitivity? Not enough shagging?

THREE – GIRLS AND LOVE AND THE UNIVERSITY AVERSION EXPLAINED. (POSSIBLY).

We've all got a book in us about our love-lives: for now I'm zooming past. It feels fair to report that I find myself flying solo, conspicuously into middle age but choose to avoid *that kind* of personal material, even though it offers the richest of all veins. This wee tome – and the two preceding volumes in this wandering #lolsobiography – are, I hope, an invitation to identify with romances of other sorts. In sport; ideas; music; art, maybe. I am not remotely afraid of exposure. I do not seek, however, indeed I do not want to compromise or embarrass or transgress against people (women or girls) that I have been deeply close to.

Aged sixteen, I was possibly not that considerate. My balls were absolutely exploding like the rest of the male population. (And, on reflection, other identities with testicles). *Moves swiftly on*.

Girls were still well behind footie – yes, I was *that* slow-off-the-mark – but alcohol and lust were suddenly players. Most of my blood *did* trammel-up into my throbbing member[21] as often as the next youth but in the contemporary idiom I had 'no technology with wimmin'. In theory parties were opportunities but mainly even then I was found wanting. (Pun intended). Groping and cavorting *did occur* but this was only possible under masses of drink; like dancing. I was almost completely inadequate and the rest was football, anyway – football and increasingly music.

In the sixth form we did get closer to girls and some of the more extravagant weirdos even made friends with them. There was one gorgeous specimen of womanhood who made me ache for two years solid. (Pun intended). She was beautiful and physically-developed in a way that took her beyond comprehension and reach – and yes, I'm afraid there's no escaping the fact that body-shape and desirability were shockingly closely associated, then and possibly now. (I was a hormonal monster aged seventeen and cannot deny the role that a certain kind of 'attractiveness' still plays in my allegedly adult life. Guilty as charged. We blokes may learn stuff about value and personality but we remain in my experience distressingly blokey. Understand that some may call out this 'confession' as a mere smokescreen for misogyny).

This girl was a stylish, witty, hugely likable individual and she was beautiful. Could be that we weren't an overwhelmingly fashion-conscious bunch, even for an underwhelmingly innocent time, but there was something undeniably chic about her barnet. I could never quite

---

[21] Think this is how said implement was described in *certain types* of literature at the time. Can't, of course, be sure.

work out what it was: angles and curves, or something. Anyway there were lots of other things going on, life was roaring around us but if it stilled, or if she was close, I was marooned in a kind of lurv-madness. I nearly found myself going out with her after a particularly drunken night in Cleethorpes:[22] but in one of those truly mind-blowing all-time gaffes I didn't follow it up. Didn't have the technology. Gone.

*

My chronology goes all out of synch on certain things and what follows is one of them. University. Before and during the process of application/interview/all that bollocks I was certain I wasn't going. (If my father had still been alive, I have no doubt this conscientious objection would not have been viable. He was no bully but I would have been levered into the next phase of academic action).

My sense of the world and The System as a fraud and of the shambolic emptiness of everything that smacked of The Clampdown was by now highly developed, via the advent of punk and the imminent pall of Thatcherism. I knew that universities were middle-class ghettos and therefore a functioning part of the production-line towards universal complicity. I did a lot of hating around these themes.

Can't be clear of dates, processes, timelines but *at some stage* and despite being privately adamant that

---

[22] I could have dreamt this. Or, yeh, just been *particularly drunk*.

I wasn't having any of this automatic school to uni to sensible job nonsense, I went for interviews at the following. Cambridge; Royal Holloway College; Nottingham University.

Our new Head of Sixth Form was a decent and sporty bloke but we barely got to speak. Then he offered two of us – me and Ed Harker(?) – the opportunity to have one of those informal, pre-application interviews with a contact of his at Cambridge University. The sort of thing that those twats from the likes of Eton or Harrow get routinely. (This was waaay before exams and exam results. I sat three A Levels and two S Levels but because my A's were so shite – A/D/E; English/Geography/Geology – my S Levels were never marked, and any Oxbridge ambitions – his, not mine – were promptly squished).

The trip to Cambridge was therefore a failed and fruitless attempt to strike a blow for the Comprehensive School Boot-boys. I can remember almost nothing of it, except a weird, charade-like conversation with some fairly disinterested geezer in a study-room. Maybe off a quad. Don't think Ed got in either but certain he would have gotten good exam grades. My eldest bro' (also State School educated, of course) got in to Oriel College Oxford[23] some time before this, so I had been to check out the vibe there. Like Cambridge, it stank of privilege.

When I found out where Royal Holloway College *was*, I was both perversely intrigued and probably determined

---

[23] On merit. Bright kid, outstanding sportsman. Oh – and of course there were some great people there.

to hate it. When I arrived and saw the dreamy bloody towers it only confirmed those prejudices against Tories and The South. I had applied to do English and must have visited before my results came out. The lecturer *definitely* wasn't interested in engaging so I may have tried to wake him up by saying something about E J Thribb. He almost stirred and I left happy in the knowledge that I would never return.

Nottingham was more interesting and more real. Plus I'd heard that the women-to-men ratio was 5-2. I had applied to do Geography with Geology, I think. I met a lovely bloke and we talked about Brian Clough for about an hour. It's possible I might even had gone there if I hadn't ballsed-up the exams.

Aeons later I can only reflect on the degree to which the Waltonian A-level debacle was a sort of self-sabotage. Where the hell *did* it sit, on the conscious/unconscious scale?

I was too splenetically angry at everything to settle into life, never mind university life. In my arrogance I knew I was brainy enough to go to college and that I didn't need anybody's stamp of approval: not 'for jobs' or for some feeble or conveniently crushing concept of what the future should look like for a 'lad like me'. Bollocks to that. College would have felt like a very early cop-out from the mad-but-heartfelt aspiration to oppose everything that smacked of Mr Clean. Therefore it was simple: I wouldn't and couldn't go.

If that's the weirdest and wildest Matter of Principle you've heard this week then so be it. That's kinda what it was. Instead of learning more about pIate tectonics or Joseph Conrad I bummed around on the dole, got factory jobs and worked in a travel agency. Then headed for Wales.

FOUR – BRIEF WALES HIGHLIGHTS: (AGAIN).

I live in West Wales, have done for 40 years, near as dammit the whole of my adult life. It remains a singular privilege. Many of my better or most heartfelt reflections on life as a Plastic Taff[24] appear in previous volumes, so this will be briefish.

Based in Pembs, I have worked for the Greatest Hotel on the Planet, then as a landscaper, then in sport, as a cricket coach and teacher of PE. I still work in cricket, on the local Regional Pathway. I have two grown-up kids, educated initially through the medium of Welsh, because to their Dad that was important 'politically' *and* because their mamgu was a habitual user of her native tongue, chiefly through her daily phone-calls with the fabulous Gwen, whom she had walked to school with in North Pembs, in the 1930s. "Ohh, Gwen bach!!"

I have never quite amassed the required wedge to facilitate purchase of a Pembrokeshire sea view (and there's no chance now!) but have bobbed and weaved so

---

[24] Thankyou, Tim Whitley.

as to remain within yomping distance. The coast – and the now renowned Coast Path – is probably why I'm here.

*

Playing for mighty Solva Athletic Football Club and years later for Llanrhian, Pembrokeshire and Wales Seniors Cricket Clubs has been and is an essential and invigorating part of my existence in the way that many of you will be familiar with. (I'm probably repeating but) hilarious. Daft. Wonderful. Utterly central to my life and social life. I may yet write more about the marvel that is team sport. But for now I want to make this a wee highlights package of New Stories which somehow gel with the lurv-joy-energy boogaboog that hopefully winds its way through this book.

It's probably 1983. I'm the barman at the Druidstone Hotel. I'm probably hungover and knackered but happy. A minibus trundles down the drive – a drive which offers some of the most sensational vistas these isles can offer. Restorative. Thrilling. Beautiful. A load of blokes start peeling themselves out of the bus. There are signs of slightly weird (slightly crappy) purplish suits, part-worn or part slung about the vehicle. People are stretching... and swearing... and *responding*.

These lads are Irish, so there are a few 'fecks' about, mixed in with the groans and sunny salutations. We do the quick hello's thing as they nudge open the waist-high gate in the low, cock-and-hen stone wall that separates the plain, rather coarse drive from the path to the beach. My memory suggests that it was late afternoon on a relatively ordinary day – I think a Sunday – but the key takeaway is that the Dru View was already working its magic.

Fellas keep on coming out of that bus. Creased and "completely shagged-out" and more or less grumpy, post the torture of the journey. They shuffle and yawn and fall through the gate until we're all inhaling St Bride's Bay in a kind of spent ecstasy – even those of us who do this for a living. "Feck me we needed this. We needed this, eh boys?"

Turns out they'd packed 15 of 'em into a 13 seater minibus; somebody had completely ballsed-up the hire-thing. Turns out they're a barber shop singing group – hence the crimplene(?) suits – who'd been at Warwick University for best part of a week, competing in some shockingly major *singing contest*. Rod Bell, the hotel owner and one of the finest blokes I've ever met, had I think some loose or wild connection with some member of the troop, although whether this was to do with mad land-yachting trips to the West of Ireland or something less tenuous I'm simply not able to recall. But they were here and it turned out just grand.

The barbershop contest was not at all what they'd expected. They love their singing but were inevitably "only there for the craic", having no real idea they were to be joined by worryingly disciplined crews from the States and all over Europe. It was a disaster of sorts: the travel, to and from County Cork; the mismatch singing-wise; their mad, unserious approach. But now they'd landed at the Dru... and they really got it.

After brief deposition of bus detritus into their rooms, and maybe one or two relieving showers, the lads started to drift down to the bar. (This remains a fabulously evocative and restful kindofa place – or will be again, when the current re-furb takes it back to where it was for many years). They took a further inhalation of the bay and trundled back in to where yours truly was stationed, at the bar-front. The news that we had both Guinness and Murphy's on tap was received quietly but warmly, as was the sight of more than one species of Blackbush and Jameson's up amongst the spirits. It began.

This started in daylight… and finished in daylight. Hard to focus entirely on the intervening period but have absolutely no doubt that it featured one of the greatest social occasions of my life. Am certain that everybody who had the staggering good fortune to be there, by accident or design, would say the same. There was a tremendous amount of wholesome drinking – and some less prudent adventures. Poteen was produced from god-knows-where. Dangerously home-made-looking poteen. Worse still, we drank it. For all its innocent, 90 per cent *clarity* (with just that slight milkiness) it was every bit the rocket fuel of the republic. It didn't so much tip you over the edge as launch you into leg-jiggling oblivion. (We did have to send out a general reminder that deadly cliffs were about four foot six thattaway when folks went 'out for some air'). Mon Dieu, bejaysus and duw bloody duw;[25] it was a session.

---

[25] God, in the Welsh, but often said like this, in my (Pembs) experience.

Oh – and there was singing. These gloriously mental Irishmen, having shaken off the journey, the assholes from Florida and their own, terminal sore-throats, started warbling about 8pm and didn't finish 'til 5 of the morning. My last and abiding memory is of the local farmer – a regular, whom of course I knew well – fluffing his version of 'Imagine' through nerves more than alcohol, because he'd only previously shared it with the dog, in the kitchen. (He later told me, genuinely crestfallen, that he'd played that song every night for about twenty years, on his own acoustic guitar. Given this was the loveliest, most sympathetic audience a man could ever ask for – and everybody in the bar was joining in to everything, *and* the fella could genuinely sing! – it's hard to imagine how ole Stuart T could fail to be carried along. But he did 'fail'. Amazingly and rather unfortunately).

Elsewhere it was like some idyll of creative comradeship. It's so long ago and there was so much libation involved that I can't for the life of me think what we were all singing: a fabulous, absurd range of things. I know it was beautiful – *they* were beautiful. They could *really sing* and we were drawn in. It transcended performance and really did become something special and generous and unifying. Sure we were mostly drunk; we were soulful drunks giving it full wallop. And on some occasions I get that this can be too much – intimidating even. Not that night. It was a kind of bliss.

*

I worked this bar for about three years. It was whilst I was playing football for Solva. I was early twenties, so fit, but initially, like so many in the trade, I worked 60 plus hours a week, until Jane, the unstoppable co-proprietor, realized this was madness. (There were lots of very unhealthy late nights: it was just the way it was). The Bells were and are like family to me: remarkable people running a unique and lovably anarchic place.

Everything comes back to people, does it not? Many of the guests became huge friends, the Dru becoming a central part of their lives in the same way that it was woven into ours. As the barman I was maybe best-placed to see just how and how many people really relaxed there, really deeply mellowed or found themselves (if that doesn't sound too unhinged?) Being a part of that felt like another quiet privilege.

I could write a list of the fabulous and interesting folks I've met or part-hosted at this extraordinary place. I won't. And for now I'm not even going to name the particular individual who becomes a key to the next adventure; he was a tremendously modest man and it just doesn't feel appropriate. I think it's a lovely story that speaks to the power of commonalities; stuff that is often intuitively shared.

This guy came to the hotel more than once, generally in the company of his family but also to escape (from London) for a long weekend or similar with an extravagant and I believe extravagantly wealthy theatre impresario. They were just mates. They were incredibly and fascinatingly different. I liked them both. Let's call them John and Robert. John, it turns out, is a world-level theatre photographer and therefore a genuine artist. We talked mainly about football – the daft bugger's an Arsenal fan.

Now I can talk about football. Even as a young man I could do that. It's really in the blood – read those other books – and I was a decent, skilful player, though not a professional. I was also writing, although I'm not at all sure that I would have shared that with John or Robert: it was certainly not my way to try to inveigle a way in to anything. We had some laughs, drank a bit and talked. It was intimate in that lovely sense of being unforced and non-hierarchical and honest, in what we now call a 'safe space' – a bar, with just a few pals knocking about.

John knew his football so talked a fair bit about Liam Brady – 'nuff sed, if you know your football and/or your Arsenal FC. (No issues; genius and one of very few players from our islands/their Ireland(?) to have built an extended and successful career in Italy. #Player).

This can be read as arrogance but stays in here: we both loved football and understood it pretty well. We both loved skill so were drawn to the great Dutch teams and, even though he was an ardent Gooner, players like Glenn Hoddle – not that there were many like him. Football *needed* to be about natural, generous expression. We said cornball stuff of that nature to each other, and to anybody else who might listen; sometimes we did it in complete sobriety.

I was coming to the natural end of my time at this hotel. By no means had I fallen out of love with it but maybe needed a change. John the ace photographer, who's life I knew almost nothing about, needed an assistant. He lived about nine foot two from where one of my brothers was living, in a run-down but homely terrace near Swiss Cottage – a cheap housing co-op-cum-squat.

John knew I had no experience *at all* of darkroom work and only a passing interest in photography. But because of the wonderful madness that is conviviality, trust and good energy, he knew somehow I'd be a good worker and a decent bloke to have around. I went to London.

FIVE – BRIEF LONDON HIGHLIGHTS.

Let me just underline how little, really, John knew about me, and therefore how fabulous, generous and rich was his gamble. We worked together, in his family house, with wife, kids and animals often present. The work was important – front of house pics and publicity stills for major London theatres. I was soon developing the film (almost always, we worked in black and white) and even printing some of the pictures, in particular the 10 by 8 inch jobs which went out to press, via theatres. Think that through: you only get the one chance to develop films... and the printing needed to be professional quality. John got me there quickly, for obvious reasons.

All this was the result of him trusting me and me trusting him. I guess he figured that somebody who understood Glenn Hoddle's genius was a safe bet. That human instincts can be good and strong. But that's still feeling like an impressive plunge, forty-odd years later.

I worked part-time for John for more than two years. Doing everything that needed doing. Freeing him up to take those brilliant pictures. Very often I would go with him to the Royal Court, Hampstead Theatre or to the

National to change films and generally assist. He would always shoot live rehearsals, usually the last one before opening, using two cameras. There wouldn't be much kit – a monopod, sometimes, and a bag with cameras, lenses and films – so we travelled light, but I could make myself useful. Sometimes I would take back-up pictures.

Later I would do more of my own work: John had deliberately made that possible by putting my face about and offering guidance in that quietly humble way of his. He put me in front of Feininger's 'Manual of Advanced Photography' and showed me Cartier-Bresson. (Anyone who knows photography will know that these are both pointers to this being an art of the soul, much more than a medium for fetishizing clobber in the way that many photographers undoubtedly do). I did a lot of watching and a lot of learning, in good time becoming the printer I needed to be to make John's trust and investment in me beneficial to both.

I may need to drop in the word 'privilege' again here. All mine. This guy was the genuine article – the best theatre photographer in the land – and a truly lovely man at the same time. He had cornered the market, pretty much, in terms of good London venues. I saw progressive and important work every week. We rarely covered commercial theatre – the fella didn't need to.

Financially I was barely getting by but this was and is no reflection on this work, which was always agreed to be two days a week. Our gaff in Hilgrove Road was splendidly feisty and full of fun but being skint in London is not easy. I was angry and I was writing and thinking about music. Thatcher and punk were in my head. The North and the South chasm was in my head.

Alongside of writing a play called 'Barbeque in Burnley' I had a couple of seasons playing football for Poly FC at the Quinton Hogg Memorial Ground, Chiswick, alongside my eldest bro'. I made some great mates there. For the lols and to try and squeeze out a bit of cash, myself and Bro 2 had a stall on Camden Market, flogging unwanted clothes from friends, mainly, decades before pre-loved became lucrative and Camden became deeply and profitably cool.

Quite late-on during my effective apprenticeship, a certain Lauren Bacall was starring – and I do mean starring – in 'Sweet Bird of Youth' – at the Haymarket Theatre (I think). For this, the Man Himself was a wee bit nervous. From memory, we didn't get the usual live run of a full rehearsal; it was more choreographed than that.

When we appeared out front John was introduced to LB. She was into her seventies but glamorous – a word which may date us both.

Bacall was both charming *and* something of a force: she asked John where he might be intending to work and then told him that 'her directors (meaning film) always shot her from above'. Apparently it was more flattering. John, who had briefly shaken her hand whilst I was a few yards back in the auditorium, was momentarily a bit flustered by this but a ladder was soon produced, from which he could then take some pics from an elevated position. She inevitably had approval on the results, symbolizing Bacall's clout in the industry. Under normal circumstances the photographer would make pictorial/editorial cuts before offering theatres or producers the choice from amongst his selections.

Rolling this memory around I note that entirely typically, my Boss Man made a point of introducing me to Lauren Bacall. John printed the pictures himself that night, working notably hard under the enlarger to keep them a) atmospheric and 'true to the piece' whilst being aware of the potentially contradictory imperative for b) keeping them *sympathetic to the actress.*

The exposure and printing of black and white images really can look and feel like sculpting. It's an undeniably mercurial process, one which I loved and became medium-decent at. I do hope to get back to it one day but this may not, sadly, be realistic.

Weirdly perhaps, though I was massively grateful for all the opportunities and camaraderie offered by John the Artist, and despite the patently electric charge that live performance provides, I wasn't that heavily inspired or even enamoured by much of the allegedly progressive theatre we were watching. Weirder still, perhaps, I was and remain more struck by and through the community theatre that I had seen back in Wales: genuinely. (I had seen and got to know Hijinx, Spectacle and other tiddly theatre posses in previous years, and later worked for the former as a photographer. They were magic, both in terms of quality and integrity). Playing your heart out to 14 people and a dog in a village hall outside Aberystwyth still gets my love and respect; not out of sentiment or sympathy but because of the quality of the work done and that whole thing of bringing culture into non-privileged places.

The Royal Court didn't feel the same, didn't feel as good, despite being the apex of radical theatre for an age. This I concede reflects the giant chips I had on my youthful shoulders as much as any critical understanding. I was angry that staff and players seemed and sounded so middle-class. That there were double-barrel names. I didn't believe these people, or believe in them. (I may have been wrong). Ironically, some time later the script for my first play was described as 'the diamond in the dung-heap' by a reader for that same establishment. That remains an important validation for me today. (Go figure – or judge?)

*

There will be a recurring theme here, to do with missed 'openings' or me being too dumb, too mischievous, too perverse and/or too network-averse to *turn myself into something*. This book almost became *primarily* an investigation into that tendency for commercial/ economic suicide. Played largely for laughs. (Hang on. Maybe that's what it is?!?) I have no regrets but will offer maybe one more example of RW the anti-capitalist or anti-opportunity maniac; simply because it's true.

1984-ish. A great friend – bezzie of a bezzie – has made herself into a Director with Real Potential. In a rare moment of insight, I see that it would be ridiculous not to send her a script I've written. She's fab; she's a talent; she knows people and has ambition. I don't, but why not send it? She is encouraging and flashes it on to various 'good theatre places'. One of the results is that I get that encouragement from the Royal Court, and – be-Jaysus – the National Theatre Studio invites me (and her, as an upcoming director) to 'workshop' the play.[26]

I think by this time I might have written or part-written a second play, which we also throw around the room with National Theatre actors. Dinah Stabb was one of them; so was Ron Cook.

Now I don't think I'm an arrogant bloke – not even then – but I recall staying at my Big Bro's house in London before that first trip into the National Theatre Studio and feeling fearless about the whole venture. Not because I thought this was or was gonna be My Territory. This wasn't and isn't, I think, about confidence. I knew the play was mad, or that it was a million miles away from standard contemporary theatre (o-kaaay whatever that is or was). I just had no fear of being judged: not by these fekkers; not by anybody. This thing was *of me* and was blisteringly honest and (I suppose) expressionistic in a way that they would either get, or not. I didn't care. I was planting my flag and fuck 'em. (I erm, still feel like this).

---

[26] There's a coruscating Alexei Sayle sketch from this era that slaughters the idea of workshopping, for its pretence. I did feel a bit that way about this whole venture. I also remember clearly fearing the cost of travel, etc. But they paid me. Rail fare plus a week's wages.

In fact I planted the Italian flag. I was wearing the shirt of the Azurri under my black denim jacket when I walked in; mostly as a way of supporting my fabulous-generous 'sponsor', the Italian director-friend. When offered the opportunity to say something about the play – which initially was 'Barbeque in Burnley', a wild fable about football and politics – I got somebody to play 'Hit the North' by The Fall. This to somehow key us in to the anti-Thatcherite (and yup, Northern) angularity of the play. I remember one young woman tapping her toes but I probably talked too much and the remainder may have thought I was off my head. I didn't care: we actually had fun – or I did. And yep I'm proud to have been the fella that force-fed them Southern Softies Mark E Smith.

Later in the day a young bloke who I learned from my director-friend 'had just been brilliant in a West End play' said he loved it and wanted to sign up there and then to play the lead character 'Boy Wunda'. Seemed a really good lad and understood when I told him BW probably couldn't or shouldn't be a Scouser – his original suggestion – because that smacked too much of predictable working-class heroics. He understood. Think his name was Billy something... or was that the part he had played?

During a break, upstairs at the venue, some other geezer was grinning just a little unsettlingly at me. I still don't know whether he was expecting me to know who he was but the moment passed and then we talked. He was (this again via my wing-woman) a world-renowned director and Shakespearian scholar, being friendly, as it turned out. He later invited me back – 'we just wanna get you in the building' – and kinda over-saw the writing of another short piece, called the Godfinder, which I wrote in the three days allotted. I got a letter from him – think I still have it – where he is generally complimentary and says specifically that he hopes to work with me on a play in the future. He was also unequivocal re The Godfinder: 'we could cast this now'.

So all this was great; genuinely great fun (coz too stoopid to feel any pressure of any sort) and even a clown like me could see there was some potential lurking. At the end of my two or three working visits, Nick Somebody, the gaffer at the time, called me in to his office. I remember him asking who my influences were. Without blinking I said Elvis Costello, John Lydon and maybe Paul Weller. He noted to me that they were a different kind of writer. I agreed but kinda held fast to the truth of what I'd entirely innocently said. I think he knew I wasn't trying to be cute or *project anything*, so fine. He concluded by saying that 'we – the National Theatre Studio – will put on one of your plays, at the next New Writing Festival'. This was also unequivocal.

It didn't happen… and I'm fine with that. Monies got cut, meaning inevitably that New Writing got cut. I didn't phone anyone up and ask them 'how things were'. Not my style and I'd already moved on, to working life and later to family life.

I honestly think I didn't need their validation – or any more of it? – and was simply or more broadly not driven to *achieve anything*. I was happy in Wales. I was and would always be some kind of writer, with or without them or anybody else. No issues. Even writers who aren't sisters are doin' it for themselves. In time, we put on a couple of my plays at the hotel on the clifftop in Pembs. Me and some mates. They were bloody spectacular, at least partly because the players did not in any sense think of themselves as arty people... before proving that they were... and that we all are. Seeing Pete (the next Major Barman) beaming with accomplishment and glee, bowing to an audience of fifty-odd friends and customers; that was what we might really call a theatrical success. And look – no darlings!

*

One final story on this. Because it's so damn sectionable it makes me smile. (It's also likely to be revealing – maybe again in a bad way).

There was and is mischief afoot in all of my writing. Early doors I am saying 'take this as seriously as you like': possibly in the hope of winning you over, thrillingly-against-expectation. (In fact now I think of this, it looks like I've been doing in the titles. So like *very up-front*. Which is surely reckless to the point of being erm, *ripe for analysis?*)

The plays were wild fables. I think both of the first two workshopped at the National were written by some geezer calling himself dr sir richard underworld-fish. (Grimsby, see?) Later some other crew used the underworld thing; and a director at the Royal Court appropriated my device – in 'Barbeque' – of having the lead protagonist throw bread insultingly or dismissively into the audience, mid-rant. So if it was madness it was also striking a few atonal chords here and there. But whatever. What makes me *actually smile* is the fact that when walking into the National Theatre Studio, probably on my second visit, there was a wee sign on one of the entrances to the working spaces. It read

'This week at the NTS.

We are workshopping 'My Kaleidoscope Says... The World Gets Better Every Day'

by doctor sir richard underworld-fish.

And Juliet Stevenson will be hosting a session on the Alexander Technique.

Laugh? I nearly bought a round. I kinda hoped whoever had the job of typing out that notice was giggling when they did it. I kinda hoped they had enjoyed the mad juxtaposition of this punky weirdo outta Grimsby and Wales doing his crazy thing, followed by that powerful moment of über-luvvieness.

Look of course I haven't got anything against either Juliet Stevenson or alternative therapies. I've since experienced plenty of those (the therapies I mean) and done so with mind resolutely and usually respectfully open. But in my mid-twenties, post you-know-what and you-know-who, posh things or *things that posh people did* were fair targets.

Before this studio schedule was posted I remember somebody from the National phoning me up to offer me a different workshop placement. Again entirely innocently I asked them what it entailed. The caller flatly described it as a writing adventure, hosted by a (named) famous female writer from the States. It would begin with some yoga. Later I married a yoga teacher. At the time of that phone call the whole fucking shooting match sounded like the worst kind of middle-class, intellectual masturbation. I politely turned it down. Interestingly, the caller quietly admitted that writing classes didn't suit everyone, and that the yoga thing sounded a bit 'Californian'. It was, as I have said, mid-eighties. Some of us wanted revolt not downward fucking dog.

SIX – ROCK STARDOM-AVOID. (1).

We've all got reasons why we didn't become a rock star – haven't we? (Or Jesus is that just me?) Come on: the Things That Got in the Road. Lack of Ways In or Mates Wiv Contacts or that whole Distance From London malarkey. All the conspiratorial cobblers that stops a raging talent like yooo/like me, from raging publicly.

Sometimes this is fair enough: we're actually crap. 'Have rhythm' but mediocre on the guitar. (There *really are* zillions of shit-hot guitar-players out there). Have words but maaybee they're just not as good as you think they are? Have too much FIRE, quite possibly, which is *theoretically ace* in the wonder-years of the late seventies but even then narrowed your options down to the independent labels, bless 'em. (Now, by the way, where is that fire? Idols, maybe, but where else?)

Then there's all the stuff in the matrix: a broadly shit industry; the toff-driven or haves-driven[27] anti-meritocracy of the capitalist universe; that overwhelming

---

[27] Did I just invent a Sociological Thing? Whatever. I mean haves as in – or opposite to – have-nots.

need to conciliate, to fall in behind whatever Bizz or career we bundled or sidled into. I fell at most of these multifarious barriers: in fact I dived suicidally bonce-first into the metherfekkers. And still would.

So despite one of my key soulbro's saying (admittedly forty years later) that *back then* he 'thought I was going to be Elvis Costello',[28] I failed life's audition – or certainly that one. Believe me I had the inflammation. And I did/do probably have the rhythm. Some blood relatives and best mates might proffer that I've always had the words. But drive/direction/help? Na.

Being an inadequate wreck might have kitted me out beautifully for a particular kind of artistic career but I was probably too lost in shock and grief to get *successfully* and/or redemptively lost in music. And I'm pretty sure I needed, or would have needed the right people around me to make it work. Plus despite all the artsy and angry inclinations, the decision was never made to pursue Route A... or B... or C, asitappens.

Strewth. Already into profoundly self-indulgent groove; forgive me. But – NO SURPRISES! – I'm gonna plough on because it *really does feel* like my wild, personal self-obsessiveness (and general shapelessness) could relate to some of you lot. Could be excusable-coz-transferable; translatable; transcendentally interesting, even. I failed at being Elvis Costello but maybe you succeeded? Or maybe my post-punk rocket-launch-failure was your lawyer or

---

[28] Yeh. O-kaaay. He might have said it *loosely*, without rilly meaning it, but...

builder or basket-maker-flunk? I love all this strangely-grinding psycho-bullshit. Let's go with it.

*

You may have an equivalent 'fail' from a different era and a different genre of activity entirely. But could be for many of us that it was that teen-plus period of our lives when the *central gambol* either happened or it didn't. That's a) pick up or choose a job time and b) move somewhere, maybe, to get stuck into it. It's hilariously unhelpful that monstrously big decisions need to be made (or feel like they do) just when we're most distracted by Joy Division, or Julie Oosit sashaying into The Lifeboat.

Perversely, probably even now I relish this idea that hormonal stuff and musical stuff were and always will be raging together at their max, compounding the issues, pitting and turning our ball-ache against unthinkably grown-up life-trajectories. Oof – the council. Oof – college then petro-chemicals. All this to the off-beat of The Fall.

*

I saw The Fall in what was then a crappy hall in Duncombe Street Grimsby, when I was about eighteen. I knew the music, loved it. They made that beery, spidery, edgy, shambolic noise that was our poetry and the flag for our spunky republic.

Mark E Smith was a Northern Myth and a Northern Monster. And like us he was drunk. We loved him because his ramblings coursed with our spite. He seemed to be leading his own mad nation *towards something*.

Surely it's true that for most of us the music we drape ourselves in is key to what we are and become? We come to reflect each other. I *looked like* a member of Joy Division or Bunnymen or Gang of Four – heavy coats, dark baggy clobber – because I felt like I was in those bands. It's become a cliché but they did speak for me. Only Gang of Four from amongst those three had any obvious political stance: the other two just chimed with authentic, contemporary soul. They were more or less deep and dealt in something thrilling and real. We were kinda proud to wear their badges – literally and in terms of style.

But our sartorial statements were chiefly about irony and anti-fashion, yes? True, like everybody, we had fallen into a wee tribe, and were therefore putting down some marker of a sort, but our solidarity (if that's what it was) felt rooted in music that was genuinely alternative and had genuine integrity. There's a great line or two[29] in a Dexy's number which may have applied to our dressing-down but am I kidding myself if I say that there's a difference between being essentially anti-fashion and being a New Romantic?

However thin this might sound, we felt our clan was individual and legit, because a) we were separating ourselves from the mass of normalcy and b) we weren't 'trying to look nice'. More pretentiously perhaps, we

---

[29] I'm advised we can't quote songlines due to copyright issues. Some of you will know the number...

felt that these bands had a kind of heft, had something real and defiantly meaningful in a matrix of shite and falsehood. Whatever. If I reel back from this moment – '79 and beyond? – to alight in the moment of punk, I may get a run-up at all of this.

I am clear that I never had torn clothes or tore them. I never wore safety pins. Don't think I wore any leather, although that really might have been down to that perennial lack of funds/lack of interest in fashion crossover. Would never then nor now wear leather trousers. Might have worn a black leather jacket inna Clash stylee but didn't. Have a big heavy leather jacket somewhere but no bomber jackets in the Walton wardrobe. Oh – except one, mid-eighties, which wasn't leather. This one of those weird and impulsive aberrations estranged from one's musical consciousness *and* – looking over the pics – any sign of taste.

I *did* have a pair of ridicu-skinny white drainpipe keks and I *did* on a few occasions wear them wiv giant black boots. Remember doing that to walk round our village and getting the 'oof' from one or two pals or family members. Broadly I think I was just too lost in sport to think out or make quasi-political statements around punk-as-fashion. Plus philosophically, I was definitely suss to the fact that gear was utterly secondary to belief. (There were plenty fake punks around, on a local and national level. I was punker than many, but this didn't mean I was gonna dress up as one).

Barnet-wise, a mohican was never on the cards. I certainly migrated towards shorter or even short-cropped hair and there was definitely some anti-hippy or pro-new wave sentiment bound up into that but again it never felt key. What did feel key was knowing the music, understanding what this meant, being true to certain alternatives.

At this point coupla specific memories dig in. One is of starting to wear my now dead father's checked sports jacket, probably from about 1979. It was baggy and in a brown tweed-like fabric, with a biggish but not too noisy check. Fairly certain I wore it on the plane to Canada a year or two later and this was certainly a flag-planting moment: getting off the plane in Thunder Bay Ontario looking ver-ry Elvis Costello. Think I was channeling and honouring my Dad, about 20 percent and projecting my left-field iconoclasm the other 80.

The other related flashback is to shuffling into the changing-room at a new football club – a kind of step up – wearing that jacket and one of the lads chirruping "you'll have to find a better jacket mush, if you want to play for this team". The banter was good-natured enough but I absolutely knew some of these Smooth Barsteds would find it a challenge. That I suppose was the point of wearing it. To say to the world that I was not any kind of Mr Clean-in-development.

I cannot separate growing-up from music, nor exaggerate the extent to which musical choices mattered, aged eighteen. We knew what we loved and why: we judged the rest pretty mercilessly. Do think that the times were conspiratorial in this, being acutely polarizing, and laying bare the choices around protest or conciliation. (Extraordinary and not a little concerning that this circle has turned. Do wonder if this means we will see an explosion of politically-engaged and committed music: Punk 2, anybody?)

It may sound unhinged to talk about integrity in punk singles or allude to some abstract codes of Higher Meaning embedded in particular songs. But if you don't hear them then maa'an the loss is yours. They're in there. From Pistols to Buzzcocks to Alternative TV. They are in there.

*

I'm guessing that some of you have a 1987 equivalent to my punky revelations. Or 2007. Although it grieves me to confess that I have drifted from my early, NME[30]-driven addiction to indie or alternative music I remain faithful to the idea that there is ALWAYS somebody out there producing true, radical, inspirational noises. I'm writing this book because not only did my immediate peer-group have a remarkable, united and penetrating awareness that reflected the power and import of our music, I kinda need to know that you do too. Or need to convert you.

The knowledge we had, about who was doing what, music-wise, felt like some value or force. It was, after all, intense, intensely personal *and* shared. And it sprang, we knew, from seminal, life-changing music. I slightly yearn for that knowledge and that sense these

---

[30] New Musical Express. Outstanding and maybe even remarkable during the punk years.

forty-something years later but simply don't know who's stirring up the universe in that way. Repeat that I do take comfort of a sort in the idea that *somebody always is*. Without that critical vanguard we're fucked.

So did Radiohead make you question everything, or was it The Replacements? Or Sly and the Family Stone? Or Pearl Jam, or Kendrick Lamar? Or is it KNEECAP? Whoever and whenever, I'm rilly hoping you found somebody that made you believe in a truth you could follow.

SEVEN – ROCK STARDOM-AVOID. (2).

In 1976 Elvis Costello was kinda shape-shifting away from pub/country rock bands towards something more current. Meaning he and/or his management felt punk coming and did the commercially-streetwise thing, however un-punk that might feel today. I was at least as aware as he was of the developing storm and maaay have been truer to its core. Or maybe, being in the throes of O-levels and CSEs, it was less necessary for me to *align myself* with anything? It's true that Elvis soon produced some of the greatest and most genuine protest songs you're ever likely to hear but I reckon I win this one for my implacable incorruptibility. *Cheesy grin emoji*.

The following year saw the release of My Aim is True, an astonishingly accomplished and beautiful and spirited record. 'Alison'[31] is one of the loveliest tracks ever committed to vinyl. 'Watching the Detectives' sounded crisp and stunningly new. It was a wise, skillfully-positioned album that spoke both to the angry-young-man meme and the great, less threatening

---

[31] I learned a passable version of Alison, on guitar. Beautiful song: great chord sequence.

tradition for smart songwriting. And, maybe despite the affected vocal on certain tracks – something that would persist whilst the need to performatively bristle did – the vocals were obviously top, top level. Muggins, meanwhile was getting top grades in the two Englishes, History and Geog, and was not displeased with his CSE Grade 3 in Woodwork. (One all).

During the winter of 77/78 Costello recorded 'This Year's Model', releasing it in the March of 1978. It remains a stellar achievement, including the edgily brilliant 'I don't want to go to Chelsea' and the driving, almost confrontational 'Pump It Up'. The album nails his combination of spirited pop and downright testiness at the State of Things. There's still a lot of affectation in the vocals – leaning into punk, or that possibility for spittle – but there's a strong case for putting it in the All-time Classics pile. I learned the twiddly guitar from 'Chelsea' and the (easy) sliding chords for 'Pump It Up'. Then got into 'A' levels, I suppose.

I was definitely writing songs by this stage but there was a gaping hole where my Attractions should have been. And in any case however brilliant my scribbles, I managed to avoid *finishing them* – a habit I have continued for erm, decades. So whilst Declan was banging out seven consecutive worldies between 'My Aim Is True' and 'Imperial Bedroom' – 1977-82 – RJW here was somewhat less productive. I did those 'A' levels then worked at Wold Farm Foods and United Biscuits, both of Grimsby.

The closest I got to the Music Scene was blasting my fringe vertical so that I looked vaguely like Costello on

the Trust album cover, then failing the audition for a
band I didn't want to be in. (Bass; sort of electro-new
romantic. I know, bit weird). There were also some like-
minded guys we knew who did have a band going: we
stumbled into a drinking session-cum-rehearsal-cum-
party one night. I liked the lead singer, Bill. At some
stage (it's really unlikely I would have been flash or
pushy in any sense) I showed him I could play stuff we
were both into, including 'Shack Up' – A Certain Ratio.
He was momentarily impressed but the moment passed.
They already had some 16-year-old prodigy on guitar;
from Doncaster or maybe Sheffield, if I'm not mistaken.
No need for another bloke playing rhythm: even if he
was Grimsby and maybe had the right kind of energy.

Years later, another whiff of opportunity. London. I
lived in a musical household and two of my favourite
blokes were knocking about. We 'rehearsed' briefly,
with your honourable host bawling his own words.
Geoffrey from downstairs said it 'sounded like Nick
Cave'. But we were pretty much making it up... and
because I couldn't immediately find guitar chords that
fitted the bass and the sax[32], we drifted. And then Other
Things got in the way.

We were knee-deep in Australians – good guys,
these – including members of Tinytown and

---

[32] This is one of ver-ry few times when I can clearly remember
feeling frustrated at not knowing how music works. Keys. I can hear
things and find them, given time, but don't know immediately which
key songs are in, or even which chords fit together. I fluffed this
potential kickstart coz I couldn't find the sequence.

Go-Betweens. Our housemate Geoff drummed with Tinytown and I think tried to get me an in with another Aussie band based in London. They were young and spunky and might have been a good fit but the one night their lead singer(?) generously invited me to check them out I either couldn't, or bottled it, maybe. May have been nothing; may have been a start. Given that my memory pitches them somewhere between Gang of Four and The Redskins (but hasn't yet reached their fucking name!) absolute madness not to have taken a look.

This almost becomes poignant because yes I do have an awareness of a boat long-sailed. I should have made some music. I should have done it when raging and fearless and young. I'm only two of those things now. Plus in October of 2024 I had an operation on my left hand, to straighten out two fingers badly folded-in by Du Pruyten's contracture. Months later I can't yet hold a fork and I'm a million miles from being able to form chords on a guitar. Am in physio[33] (and going through the pain barrier, believe me!) but it's entirely possible that my guitar-playing days are completely done.

So Brother MacManus has shaded this. I had his energy but failed to execute. I thought 'New Lace Sleeves' but he wrote it. Our lil' gang of Real Punksters embodied

---

[33] The day I wrote these words I'd had physio. Hurts like hell. I'd also signed up to double the amount of physio – to once a week, not once a fortnight – to try to make some inroads. I'm a philosophical guy but this is a test.

the spirit of the electrifying bands of the time – and the whole Independent Record Labels cowabunga – but he put 'Shipbuilding', 'Man Out Of Time' and 'I Want You' out there into the world. There are over 30 Elvis Costello albums: every single one of them worthy of your finest attention.

EIGHT – POLITICS FROM NOWHERE.

Now might be as good a time as any to reach back into the dark shape-shifting cupboard that is my memory around politics, or those key influences or influencers I imagine we all must have. (Not that we had that word). I don't want to itemize individual events a) because I can't be that certain of the weight of particular triggers and b) it wouldn't feel true to the mess that is or was our stumble towards *views*. I am simply clear that I went from being a relatively sheltered lad, from a loving and politically-neutral home[34] to screaming inside. And not just me. I had a soul-brother-in-anger whose rage mirrored my own: plus all those noises outside.

There was a kind of historic discontent brewing through the seventies that led somehow inevitably to everything from the deliberate and spiteful decimation of industrial communities to the rise of racism on the streets and the Poll Tax riots. Thatcher presided over the later period like some brazen, deluded queen. To us she was a bigot

---

[34] We were all about sport. Parents disengaged from politics. Dad conservative with small c. Mum arty and generous. Tolerant, enthusiastic, giving people.

and worse. We hated her for the shameless propping up of apartheid, her transparent fauxness and for doing the math around North and South. Never has the prioritisation of wealth and prosperity in the latter led to so much fury in the former.

Thatcher bought her election wins with targeted 'booms', with 'tough talk' and ugly but streetwise tribalism. Her tribe was that potent mix of gammon and suits. Some may think it bad taste or bad politics to include below the blog I wrote after her death in April 2013. But it's here because it captures what many of us felt and maybe therefore offers an insight into some of the drivers for you-know-what.

(Note for pedants: my chronology is out in the sense that the origins of punk pre-date the Thatcher Years in government). But guess what? I see on the Twitters, this very day – Feb 11th 2025, as I insert this note – that Thatcher became leader of the Conservative Party *on this day*, in 1975 (so fifty years ago). This is why we are seeing shedloads of tv/plays/films/media about her now and during the coming months. My response to this is to repeat and reaffirm that much of the disaffection and protest in society *built* alongside divisions caused by her stridency, illiberalism and outright prejudice. So no backward steps on how we regard her – then and now. She was central to our youth explosions.

Stand Down Margaret.

APRIL 9, 2013 ~ BOWLINGATVINCENT ~ EDIT

So she finally did step down from that jewel-encrusted carriage; her head dizzy with accolades, with glorious confusion, the baying crowd perceived as purring kittens to her leonine, English majesty. She descended smoothly, unaided, to some lavender field – it should be stiff with barley? – in that singing niche of her memory that for her, forever, might be if not Ingerland, then *Grantham*. And as she walks, from that shop, from that street, into the butter-cupped facsimile of that rural idyll, the parting crops do then draw up to attention... and the birds stop... and the limp sun stills above the willow. Because (she thinks, or somebody thinks) something major has happened.

And maybe it has – unless I dreamed it? Maybe there was an event as well as a death. Maybe we have to concede that? And then... in what way do we rejoice?

A rake of us – a simmering multitude with every bit as much gumption and fight and 'conviction' as she – many of us recoil from both that faux English idyll and the idolatry, the (in our view) slightly weird, slightly perverse adulation for this woman. A woman we link to some blanched – or maybe that should be scorched? – Englishness. A brutalist and therefore hugely uncultured (opposite of) outlook. A leadenness too; dull and grey and introspective in the worst of ways – bigoted, actually – reeking memorably of contempt for the most fundamental human rights in say... South Africa, as though Apartheid itself was some acceptable province of this Way We Were nation. (Mrs Thatcher, remember, *led* when it came to propping up the dying racist regime in the pre-rainbow nation. Should we celebrate the memory of *that*, I wonder?)

Even those of us who happen to be blokes, who think it was kind of great that a woman got to be PM are denied the possibility of respecting this woman. Most of us knew already, pre the coiffured barnet, accent and *manner* that Thatcher's obvious bitterness, that vile and one-dimensional and utterly hypocritical (no apology for labouring this one!) 'conviction' against the trackie-wearing classes, The Immigrants and The Homosexuals would make many of us squirm with shame or rage. The fact that she blew a historic opportunity for Britwomankind by being an utter and malevolent donkey in the role of PM has almost passed us by, such was the magnitude of her dislocating pomp.

She was sexless and yet quasi-regal, love-fodder for the dumb fawners and the prejudiced. The Mail invented her surely – she must have been pressed out of a centre-page special entitled Ideal Dictators? I can't explain her any other way. The thought of her (and I know it ain't jus' me because we've been talking, right?) simply does my head in.

She got at us personally, I suppose, one way or another. In my case, we were yeh... *close*. Having been born and spent the first twenty-odd years of my life in Grimsby, I moved to London to work as a photographer's assistant in what is atmospherically describable as The Thatcher Era. I had no money and shared a room in a rundown, terraced housing association gaff with one of my brothers. Hilgrove Road. It was great yet completely crappy in a way that we didn't mind but that made parental visits unthinkable. Stepping outside the door though and walking the couple of hundred yards up to Swiss Cottage was a revelation to this particular smalltown boy. I had never really seen posh motors – Porsches, Jaguars, Rolls Royces – down here it was crawling with them. How did that work?

Now I know this car thing may not stand up as anything other than duff anecdotal opinion but it had real meaning for me, it was true – it became truer, in fact – that there was money here in a way that had never remotely been suggested Up North. Moreover as this admittedly crass osmosis of the divisive character of Elite Southness became better enriched by my experience/observation, so my political and I think philosophical oeuvre cobbled itself together; directed (if cobbling can be directed?) by Thatcherism. It became obvious that the most humungously cynical fix was going on; put simply, that the Tories were fixing it for The South. Because it didn't matter in terms of votes or constituencies or voices how much mithering The North got up to... the South, under Thatcher won out. A massive and indeed overwhelming number of safe Tory seats in the London area effectively farted in the face of the rest.

We all knew that was what was going on. Politicking of the rawest and most unsophisticated kind. Parliament entrapped. Toffs and Tories flicking a superior brand of the V's, whilst busloads of Home Counties-returning coppers flashed their wage packets at incandescent miners. It was deeply ugly; a legacy I was reminded of last night when a friend, having howled when the subject turned to a possible State Funeral, suggested a burial more appropriate, in her view.

Sling the old witch down a fackin' mine-shaft.

(And yes, for the record, my friend is an Essex girl. And yes, she would be right in wanting me to point out that I AM AWARE poverty and discrimination existed in the South too during this period but I stand by my identification of a very real North-South divide – construct or function though that may have been of a regional and possibly parochial standpoint. And she is with me and I am with her on the notion that Thatcher quite deliberately set us against each other... and incidentally, what does that remind you of?)

Recently (and here I'm not speaking of any reactions to the death – I'm avoiding media on the subject pretty entirely) there appears a rather sickening fashion for *appreciating* Mrs T's determination and commitment to things she believed in. I'm not having that. Why credit the prejudices, the immoralities in fact, of a world leader in bulldozing folks apart? My most crucially politically-formative years were spent in a great city-state which barely acknowledged the existence of Another Country out there. Or more exactly knew all about it but didn't give a toss. Because an allegedly strong woman was making allegedly tough decisions. I came to see her then and over time as a shrill weakling; a brittle, thin-blooded creature who plastered on thick the slap of bravery and 'conviction'. I never believed a word – and I still don't.

So there.

Let's finish this wee rupture with a thought that arises. Does the vaguely commensurate (but o-kaay, maybe even more wildly dumb and amoral) Trump-Musk coalition-thing stir similar levels of outrage and disgust, amongst us Vaguely Decent People? If so, are we – or our youngsters, our off-spring – getting into the garage with guitar/drums/bass?

NINE – SINGER-SONGWRITERS VERSUS PUNK THEORY.

My instinct is not to over-think things, so I've not really *broken down* the connection I feel between Noel Coward and General Pinochet. Or Nick Drake and Michael Heseltine. Or maybe Dylan Thomas taking elocution lessons... and the CEO of Morgan Stanley. But there's something in there about privilege and conciliation being quietly vile, in its ease. Easy living; easy listening; easy-peasy. All those accommodations. All that poshness. So *preservation*. So luxury and evil.

The wild-but-near extension of this is that after a couple of pints I might argue anyone who wants to 'crack America' – everyone from the Beatles to the Clash – is committing an unpardonable sin: that of capitulation. That's what real punksters were bawling[35]. And in their anger and their genius they knew that everything 'made for radio' and tuneful and easy-on-the-ear was shite. Commercial ambition was shite. Picking acoustic guitars or playing flutes was shite. Singer-songwriting *itself* was almost certainly shite.

---

[35] Hmm. They were – we were – that's what we were saying but maybe, yaknow, without *saying it*. It was absolutely in the ether but hard to identify who made, or who could have made that argument.

This is BIG, I know. Big and wild and daft – the idea that the whole of singer-songwriting could or should be dismissed en masse. It makes me laugh to think that I can and have and often kinda do make this complete non-argument my argument: or would be stoopid enough to actually put it in a book, even a book as reckless and juvenile as this blighter. But I do, and I am. *This is how it felt.* The time for middle-class wannabee romantic poets was done. The supergroup mentality – to write for posterity, for rock greatness – was done. This was a new energy, a new art school, without the art and the schooling. Life *is* a drink and you (*do*) get drunk when you're young.[36]

*

Just pre-punk, I maybe listened to a bit of Kate Bush and Joni Mitchell. (Actually, these are shocking examples, because of course they have always been worth listening to *despite that musicality and that lyricism*) but even these gals needed a kick up the arse. To their credit, they may have understood that – appreciated it, even. Kate was both an original *and* absolutely neck-deep in the mores of the industry: groomed into it. 'Wuthering Heights' was both shockingly new and strangely necrophiliac: like yet another Period Drama. Plus Kate was undeniably art-school. I mention her because she was HUGE and she criss-crossed a zillion boundaries, including the one between integrity and sales.

---

[36] No I'm not quoting. Because you can't. Used to love The Jam, though.

Punks identified anyone who sounded like The Bizz, or was complicit in its pitches as the enemy. This was of course almost everybody. If you swam complacently along with the major record labels, the machinery of production and the Gods of Commerce then you were traitorous filth: all of you. If you deliberately made your musical sound easy to access, you were shameless, vacuous scumbags. Plus energy. If your energy was that traditional thing aspiring to loveliness and sweet diversion then you were, despite your smashtastic success, a joke.

'Rumours' is widely regarded as one of the greatest albums ever recorded. Within days, or weeks, or months, we viewed it as one of the moments that made punk *necessary* and valid. It could barely be more middle-class, more highly-polished, more brimful of desperation to be cast forward into the pantheon. Listen to them talk; listen to Pink Floyd talk and Pete Townsend talk and David Bowie and Mick Jagger. Cracked Actors from the same school – toffs of a sort, to us. Inflated and deluded and cast, for all their differences, in the same self-important mould. Closer to druggy indulgence and conservatism than real or subversive art. Ripe for an almighty kick in the bollocks. This is how we felt.

We needed punk coz supergroups. We needed punk coz the rise of Thatcher. We needed punk to sort the offensive vacancy of the commercial mainstream and to stir up or ideally get rid of these smug, well-spoken wankers.

Pretty music was out of bounds, for us: it's saccharoidal nonsense. Worse, it's conciliation from first to last. The purpose of music (in 1977/78/79) had to be sharper, more focused and actually more philosophically generous than being adorably lovely or skilled. Suddenly and thrillingly music needed and even had a responsibility to reflect and/or change our world. No room for twiddlers and idling superstars. No place for anybody 'loving that solo', 'storming up the charts' or 'finding their groove'.

*

I am an individual describing one experience, one view. But, despite knowing how off-centre it is, and noting to the universe that there is mischief here, some of it wilful, I maintain that this atomized bile-fest accurately represents much of punk theory – something that did exist, despite being pretty much un-voiced. We did and do feel these mad, ridicu-elitist (but also de-mystifying) things. We hated the indulgence and the falsity and the overwhelmingly masturbatory nature of most of the popular music in the public sphere. And we were right. The world needed what we now might call 'a re-set'. It needed three angry chords.

*

It's a stretch, I accept, to say that all music that lacked or lacks a sociological purpose (as opposed to therapeutic aspiration towards bliss) is meaningless but as a way to knock art forward, and keep yourself on your toes, I still kinda go with it. What are these guys saying? Who is it speaking for, or to?

This drive towards meaning is not a recipe for fascistically-patrolled solemnity – quite the reverse. New Wave music (again we're blurring or obliterating the boundaries) was probably characterized by its *wit*, despite the essentially moral force behind it[37]. Yes, We Who Raged demanded relevance but we understood that great pop was and is achievable, particularly if you strip out pretence or pretentiousness.

The three chords and less than three minutes thing that punk was predicated upon is very pop. It's also obviously anti-indulgence... and therefore may be supportive of smart choices. Knowing is everything: this includes knowing there is nothing wrong with 'music to wash up to'. The two poles of what we might call engaged or protest songs and ephemera can absolutely subsist – and did. 1979 may have been the peak of the history of popular music – albums and singles – because of the energy and drive of punk and the sparkling wit of energized pop.

You may have noticed we've barely nodded as we flew past the idea of entertainment. This is because punk was obviously right to demand more. Tell us something about (y)our lives. Prove to us that you really care. Pass the integrity tests; show us you're a good deserving human trying to do good. Do that thing through the

---

[37] Yes. Do mean that. 'I Did You No Wrong!' 'Career Opportunities'. 'We Are All Prostitutes'.

new wave of music; either by thrashing out your protest or via sharp, knowing but unpretentious pop. *Add value* to our entertainment.

Depending upon your view of this, I am either stuck or rooted in this period. Defiant that music is better than sugar, but accepting of the possibility for glorious trash. I'm still the bloke who can't listen to Nick Drake (etc, etc) because that's so abjectly easy on the ear. Pop can still strike me as wonderful – particularly if it revels in throwing itself away.

There really are matters of intelligence and integrity in play, here. We punksters were taught or assimilated that music should probably be visceral and sharply emotive but it can be 'light' and 'dancey' and still work. The Human League produced some truly great pop songs: songs which told real stories and sat legitimately alongside new wave music. Even if half the punks and all the rockers hated them for being 'plastic'. Phil Oakey had several daft barnets but a big heart. And you could hear it in the songs.

*

Could be a pret-ty extremist view of what constitutes legitimate music-making is being propounded here. And I don't want to roll back too far from its feisty, prismatic core – which is so obviously *of its time*. But if we twist the kaleidoscope around a little we might concede that our intensity, being rare, was (ahem) perhaps exclusive or excluding of too much. Our colours were hot and angry and sharply-defined. Youth. Hormones.

Drink. Bad People With All The Power. We needed to rip it all up.

Ordinary songs colluded against us. We had to oppose them. This was our Inspired Madness and it was also the fabulous, dynamic charge that made punk and new wave great.

TEN – GUITARS ARE WONDERFUL... AND EASY.

As I write, *clunkily* – that's with the usual ineptitude *plus*, on account of the aforementioned op on my left hand – I'm casting the proverbial longing look or twelve at my bro's classical/Spanish and my own precious Ibanez acoustic lain artfully-casually against the back wall. (Yaknow; just in case somebody drops in).

Ironies have piled-up, as they do. I've recently gone public (well, told my daughter) that I'm a) gonna get good on the guitar and b) may 'do some music' because I both want to really get that hand going – for cricket, for life – and because there remains a box to be ticked around songwriting/performing. [38]

---

[38] OK. Books take months to write. The pendulum around my hand op has swung from determination towards full re-hab (and therefore rock n roll) to concern I may not play the guitar again. Of all the things I/we should have done – and therefore of all the regrets that can clutter up our lives – not being musical in public is the biggie, for me. (I've said this out loud in order to force myself towards it. We all do that, yes?) It may not be possible. If you see me supporting Paul Weller at the Barbican, you'll know the physio did its thing.

Memory will often fail me but I reckon the very first guitar I got was what we used to call a 'cheapo'. A bad electric stratocaster copy. Twenty-odd quid job; secondhand. A Christmas present, when I was (I dunno) about fourteen? I didn't see it coming and was authentically chuffed and excited to receive it, even though it was patently 'entry level'.

Think this was the Christmas that Rajni the very temporary kitten ran up the curtains but a) I've told this story before and b) maybe on reflection I can't be certain, either about my age, or the confluence of geetar and wildcat. (Maybe it feels an attractive combo: one that could be storied?) Anyway, the guitar *was* generously given – imagine the fucking row I was likely to produce – and it was a way in.

Again I have to thank and offer up respect to my parents, on this. Looking back, there have been so many bold and generous and properly-inspired moves, from their quarter. No way could they fluke them all... and yet am I conscious that they were Great Thinkers, or expressively right-on? No. I don't remember *those kinds of conversations* taking place in front of us. (Yes we did have family quizzes, about countries, capitals, rivers and Ladybird Books of this and that were put in front of us but – even if this sounds bit freakish now – there was no sense of parental *campaigning*).

Perhaps I under-estimate them still. They were certainly fabulous, instinctively generous, intuitive people, who *modelled* good behaviours. Like skillful teachers. Like good parents. Maybe there was more strategy in play than I/we – the four lads – could imagine.

Think their gift pre-dates my incredi-passion for music/ changing the world and am pret-ty certain they couldn't feel or have any sense of the developing punkstorm, so this was wonderfully astute, or intuitive, or something. I'm not at all sure I was giving off much creative or artsy energy, at this time, other than scribbling the usual juvenile cobblers. De-facing school work-books with 'witty' epigrams; maybe writing the odd poem or lyric – discreetly, I thought. For an electric guitar and a wee battery-powered amp to drop into my lap was MASSIVE. It was also wonderfully timely and appropriate to the incoming three-chord mania.

There *was* music in the family culture. Mum was and is still at 88 a natural pianist and studied art and music alongside education, at college. More recently, a proud an-mebbes weee-bit sentimental son has been known to post vids of her playing her go-to pieces – Beethoven's 'Pathetique' and Arlen and Yarberg's 'Some Day Over the Rainbow'. She plays both from memory, despite having no memory. Not note-perfect, by any stretch, but hey, lotsa notes, and always played with feeling and no little panache, even now. Standing next to her, rolling through those keys, with the family pics and a lifetime supply of bric-a-brac on the walls, is quite the experience. Emosh.

*

Mum has spoken many times of inheriting the artsy gene from her father, the godlike Mighty Vic, who could 'do everything', including compellingly tickle the ivories. Speaking as a sports coach, I am well-familiar with the arguments around hereditary skills – 'talent'; the gene pool versus environment and opportunity or culture. I have absolutely no doubt that circumstances play a massive part in the development of our skills – artsy, sportsy or otherwise. But I am just as certain that my mum, raised in a very working-class environment where there was only occasional time or support for musical indulgences, *inherited* something.

At the next generation, my three brothers all got levered into piano lessons at some stage but somehow, (again the mechanics of this are a mystery), I flatly refused. Can't say with any confidence whether this means I got Special Treatment or if I was just an exceptionally stubborn bastard, aged eight. I remember being immovably against. Think this had something to do with a weird, almost primeval aversion to *having lessons* so as to learn to read music, which even then felt like a kind of deathly trap; a closing down of freedoms. Madness, quite possibly, but I've always registered that kind of fixed learning as anti-creative – as *suffocating*.

Know this is quite a grown-up argument: it of course figures alongside the genuinely punky anarchism that grew in my soul in '76/77 and beyond. Can't tell you how I came by it in time to philosophically oppose piano. Truth is (obvs) that I didn't. Or I certainly couldn't articulate it for the specific case of the music lessons at this time in my life. But I certainly did have a powerful and kinda free-range sense of creating music and whatever else *my own way* from about the age of fourteen/fifteen.[39] I still have that, too.

*

Anyway, the *actual playing*. No teacher, so where to start? Mainly by listening hard to vinyl and to radio – not that there was much on't wireless worth listening to, given the few available options and the overwhelming dominance of The Charts. (For the killer view on this, check out 'Radio Radio', Costello, from 1978. Spectacular deconstruction of the mainstream musical landscape. A genuinely subversive and stand-out, articulate pop song. As so often, the fella was right. You had to wade through appalling, anaesthetising crap to find stuff that was real and resonant).

Over a period of years (and yes it probably will take years) I got half-decent at finding riffs or chord sequences. Not exceptional, my playing has never been tricksy or top level and I've never wanted to be a Lead Guitar Hero but I think I can boast that I do have a reasonable ear. I can find stuff. (Some folks *do*, and *can*, yes?) That ability, to really listen and *convert*, has been at the root of any learning – that and the sheer man-hours.

So yes I chose not to learn to read music and this may again have been anarchistic stubbornness but it's always felt more fascinating and more fun this way. It's by no

---

[39] Bugger. Probably no escaping the fact that I have to offer grievously bald factoids here: born November 1960.

means a recommendation but I have loved learning and playing inna classic trial and error stylee, with the baseline of that decent ear, rather than knowledge of notes or frets on the guitar being the springboard.

Hilariously, on reflection, I did get a copy of Bert Weedon's[40] 'Play in a Day' to nudge me along. Despite ole Bert looking like some dubious uncle and being, I think, American.

The guy seemed MASSIVELY, cheesily uncool – not that I/we would ever use that word – too American and therefore kindof unthinkable for us at this time. (Still feels faux, in fact, despite the cultural onslaught). He had little to offer a proto-Weller except a couple of introductory twiddles and a slack handful of essential chords. (So in fact I did learn some entry-level stuff, before dispatching him promptly under the bed or into the depths of the cupboard; before the Local Youff came round).

I'm straining here, but could well be Bert included a sort of idiot's guide to 'Three Blind Mice' as a firestarter. Oh yeh. Later I would find a temporarily dude-ish equivalent – the same one used by a million budding Blackmores. 'Smoke on the Water'.

---

[40] Can't honestly be arsed to google him but Bert was a sort of stalwart guitar player/tutor, somehow projected into the world's consciousness. Dunno how or why. But he was the man parents went to get their kids started on the guitar. With 'Play in a Day'.

God that makes me smile. Dud dud daaa, dud dud du-derrr; dud dud daa, dad-daaa! On the bass string then using chords, over frets 0 (open), 3, 5 and 7. Hilarious – and suddenly sentimental. (On a recent return to Up North, over a couple of lunchtimes sherberts, the mighty Wayne Okopskyj – early soul-brother, Ukrainian family, 42 years in the British army – reminded me that I taught him this riff. Man we laughed!)

In truth I never liked that 'heavy' shite for more than about five minutes but that thundering riff was so everywhere and so easy and (on my wee amp) so *punchy* that being able to sound like a rock star for those few deluded moments did have its attractions. I repeat: as soon as more than three of my braincells energized – about 1975, maybe – I cast the cock rock dullards and the virtuoso glory-seekers the feck out of there.

Anyway, Comrade Bert did provide some chords and it was patently obvious, even to a klutz like me that just a few of them would get me where I wanted to be. Then it would be down to practice... and noises offstage.

*

If you get an electric guitar you probably do need an amp; the fekkers hardly make a noise without, having no effective 'body'. I got a box about nine or ten inches high and six across. Given that even this, at full volume, would spoil your Sunday dinner no problem, it was hugely generous of mum and dad to go there – either that or simply naïve, of course. It also had a fuzzy, genuinely attacking sound, which did contribute to the direction of travel. The batteries weren't cheap, so I kept usage to a minimum, but it was exciting to find riffettes or begin to crunch out some authentically clean chords... and let 'em flood the airspace.

You *need to learn* A and D and E and E minor and B minor and G and C. That really may be enough. F I suppose gets you into the F/G/B flat/C zone, which is also rich territory in terms of rock and roll history and material sequences. But you *have to* put the hours in, maybe especially on steel strings, because you have to harden your fingertips. If you're not making them sore, early-doors, you're not being brave or committed enough. Every day, an hour or two and within a week or a fortnight you can really go at it. So go at it.

(Hark at me, giving it the Musical Authority thing but) maybe find a couple of simple riffs – could be a nursery rhyme, could be Joy Division – and play the hell out of them. Start blocking across strings, for example just the one finger (probs the first) to play the chord of A, and then get onto bar chords ASAP. But hold up: I'm forgetting how much the world has changed.

T'internet. Learning has (wow) been transformed. Now you can find eight zillion guitar tutors and forty billion 'helpful videos' online. And they *are* helpful – or can be. You can do it without (and in some ways that feels lovelier) but why wouldn't you look for the words and the chords of your favourite songs and then hack away at them? Why wouldn't you? That too could be a magical process. Find the songs you love and look hard at the chords. Learn them. Learn the sexy geetar riffs if you want. Spend aeons or spend minutes: just get to the place where you can play a *recognizable version*. Sing your fucking heart out or mumble – or just play your guitar.

Repeating unashamedly. It really may be a wonder of the world that you can now, within seconds, find words, chord-shapes and even some geezer in Minnebloodysota plinking out your favourite song – the anthem to your life or the thang you want to have sex to. Wonderful. Soon as my hand heals I'll be back on there, looking for more Cure, Bunnymen or Longpigs. It's a ravishing musical short-cut, this googling.

*

There's no doubt that my foaming commitment to punky-minimalism entrenched my conviction that chords are where it's at but receipt of my first guitar *did* pre-date punk, so I'm left with the non-conclusion – for it's all ver-ry vague, this – that maybe my reasonable propensity for rhythm nudged me irreversibly towards erm, rhythm guitar. As opposed to joining the needy virtuosos playing lead. (Just joking, lads! Or however you identify! *Thumbs up emoji)*.

The Ramones went on to triumphantly bludgeon the three chord mantra into music history but though I absolutely get behind the Simplicity As Opportunity/ De-mystification Is All schtick, this is but one of the Powers of Punk, yes? It's good – no, great – that **we can** *all do this.* It's thrilling and right that we can *reclaim storytelling from the Gifted and Talented* (or those who have a way in). But re my own specific Guitar Journey, I suspect I didn't turn into a rhythm guitar player for overwhelmingly philosophical reasons. Oh no. I just loved strumming.

I may be *anti-technique*, in my soul. That may be true. I may be drawn to the poetry of movement as opposed to the execution of skills in most things. (Hmm: *author pauses performatively, for thought*). Particularly where the execution somehow implies exhibitionism, at any level. Plus chords sound good; there's a strong sense, maybe particularly on the acoustic, that you just don't need anything else. (I suppose the electric equivalent is 'power chords': and maybe the sense is there, too. It's just in a different sonic register, ma'an: punchier, edgier, more viscerally engaging, perhaps?)

So I guess I'm saying that not only is there no shame in 'aiming low', towards being a mere rhythm guitar merchant like my good self, there's whole lotta joy. Work at it. You can go on to being a twiddlemeister from there, should you want. And being 'limited' doesn't mean you're limited to knocking out punk anthems. Mercifully, the universe is full of ver-ry simple songs.

*

Some further axe-anorakdom. It may even be helpful.

It will take weeks not days but as soon as you have mastered clean strings and are using bar chords you're absolutely flying. Not only are all the wee extras awaiting discovery – minors, majors, sevenths, sustained fourths, the whole delirium-inducing cowabunga – but you can suddenly play a version of every song ever ever.

Barring across the strings makes a new world of adapted chords easily available. (It's a revelation, you wait). And the blocking or chopping or ringing of the chords opens up a fabulous vocabulary of playing. Get your finger across; flatten out the buzzes and the wails. Bully your way through the grief.

Some axe-merchants get their thumb over and down into bar chords. This seems to me like a goodish idea – Weller was one clear and attractive exponent – but I never did it and I'm not sure I could get there now. It may free up fingers and there's something undeniably cool[41] about that grip on the neck. (*Thinks*: perhaps this is a good mini-project for my post-op rehabilitation?)

There are times when I think barring via sole use (as it were) of my first finger, left hand, *may* restrict playing but ach, I'm not convinced. Skillful and well-timed chord changes literally make the music, or feel more important, alongside sympathetic strumming. This stuff doesn't lend itself well to 'analysis' in any case, so let's go with a very personal and unscientific hunch that it's the strumming that carries things, makes the choon *work*, maybe particularly on the acoustic, whatever chords or picking style you may be using.

---

[41] Feels ok to use that word here. (Go figure).

Oof; biggish contentious socio-philosophical wotsits upcoming. This conviction (or at the very least, large hairy suspicion) that 'being a natural' and having flow or rhythm *is* important, is *at the same time* tenuous. And maybe not very punk – regrettably. But I'm afraid it could be true that whilst you can *unquestionably improve these things*, you may be bollocksed, ultimately, if your strumming is crap.

Recollections are blurry as to what I learnt and when and which songbooks were bought, in the early years. A couple of chord books – that is, books with just lists of chords or 'chord shapes', generally gathered into families or keys, with dots and/or numbers showing finger positions on the fretboard – were essential and did indeed appear. As with all things, there is no short-cut here: you have to put the man-hours in and the rewards *will* come. You do need to learn to change chords seamlessly and quickly – so practice. You do need to get comfortable with certain chord sequences – so practice.

I may be scooting forward and not accounting for gaps if I report that amongst the chord books I bought or was gifted were: Jam and Clash songbooks; Elvis Costello songbooks – including a comprehensive anthology, which I am suddenly compelled to return to, as part of what I am now thinking of as my Rehab Re-boot.

There were Police and other post-punk or indie band songbooks; or in many cases individual songs lifted or photo-copied from or by brother Jes. Talking Heads featured pretty strongly amongst these: the brilliant slidy-but-crunchy guitar on 'Life During Wartime' and the power chords on 'Psychokiller' were faves that I found passable versions for. The simple but soaring riff on Joy Division's unassailably mighty 'Transmission' also got my juices flowing. I found key chords for several JD songs, including 'Shadowplay' but have skirted around 'Love Will Tear Us Apart, despite the strumtastic guitar: maybe because it's just too obvious and too over-represented on Youtube videos or wannabee versions.

Years later I was given a 'Heart-shaped Pool' (Radiohead) songbook but it's ahead of where I'm at, as a player. I still get copies of things now and then, mainly from said brother, but even pre- op I was bloody awful at keeping up with that long-established level of competence. You don't lose it entirely but life and family life can really get in the way of your guitar-playing moments. Fair enough – and no complaints.

ELEVEN – PROPER PUNKS: WHO, THEN?

But enough of this playing malarkey. A re-cap of the spirit of things, when this teetering youth was first getting top-side of those chord-changes.

Ninety percent of the industry was working for the clampdown... and insiders to the bizz or no, we *judged* the fekkers. If they were BIG, it could only be because they were farming their fame and their shallowness. If they didn't speak to us of the now, the angry now, with its wild but politically-charged, intellectually-focused urgency, they were the enemy. If they had no sense of the fury we sensed, they were the enemy. In this way punk was both magnificently cleansing and paradoxically elitist. In our opinionated rage – the land I still call home – we were massively and even morally right. But though we energized the whole universe, we were flawed, and reckless, and clumsy.

Like almost every movement you could call to mind, we lacked voices – or we rarely heard the articulate voices. Of course the media and the system conspired against them but none of Lydon nor Strummer nor Weller nor Siouxsie had the wherewithal to make good, sustained arguments. A) They were young. B) They were using plenty drugs. C) They were flawed people.

Why in any case, would it be their job to do anything beyond rage, in their various, magnificent ways? They were absolutely united in representing something – something powerful and culturally significant – but don't ask 'em to explain it all to Melvyn Bragg. Whilst it's incontrovertibly true that punk (and beyond) was historically energising and populist (in a good way), and we can now pin compelling theories to it, around the demystification of art and the rights of the masses to be heard and valued, it was largely, rightly and necessarily, a fucking racket, badly-explained.

I've said or implied that I'm less interested in history than in feeling. This is surely because of the ravishing subjectivity of our views on any kind of art and the tribal cobblers that gets in the way of fact. It may be that we have our American brothers and sisters to thank for the genesis of punk. But a) I don't want to believe that and b) I am clear that MC5 – to quote one much-vaunted protagonist – were so deeply into lead guitar and girlie haircuts[42] that they can't be taken seriously as progenitors. Plus our punk felt very British. Plainly there were honourable and early contributions from both sides of the Atlantic – and from the likes of Australia, if the truth be told. Who you believe in depends on who you like and where you're from.

---

[42] Yes. I am being *deliberately offensive*. They made a bloated, indulgent noise.

Here in Blighty us Northern Lads would never accept that punk was all about London but of course the Lydon-McLaren-Westwood triumvirate was central. Weird how Kings Road CHELSEA, about four foot two from SLOANE SQUARE could ever be a starting-point for a class-conscious cultural rebellion but it was. A shop called 'Sex'. A 'puppet-master'. A bloke called Rotten. The idea that The System and The Music Bizz was filth, so fight it with phlegm. And turn that phlegm into anthems. And turn the anthems into slogans or t-shirts, or vice-versa.

McLaren may have been a monster or a genius; he was certainly an entrepreneur. In that sense he made things possible – he put them out there. Purists of a sort may argue that he was a capitalist and a leech and that the music could have happened without him but... it didn't... and it happened. However right it might feel to make this 'all about the music' it's important to note that there's a viable argument that punk rock came out of (or is unthinkable without) punk fashion. Westwood and McLaren *were* important.

Lydon was and is somewhere between the various caricatures of force of nature, clown and cultural icon. He was and is punk, for better and worse. For all his loudmouthery and those moments where we Guardian-reading liberals had wished he would 'just stop!' Lydon has produced material of staggering ambition and import. (So I for one largely forgive him). The Pistols singles are almost as sensational now as they were then. 'Public Image' the single is an extraordinary and well-executed re-birth. 'Poptones', 'Careering', 'Flowers of Romance', 'Keep Banging the Door' and 'Rise' are all giants.

When 'Anarchy' arrived, it's not hyperbolic to describe it as the ringing of some division bell. It was a statement of defiance and newness. It was a challenge that battered into living-rooms and subverted lives. That song, that *moment*, despite the undeniable whiff of punk fashionista around it, was MASSIVE. It remains one of the Great Noises.

But don't read me arseing on about what new wave was challenging and how. Listen to that fucking chunk of vinyl. Even now. The explainers become redundant. I can't quote the lyrics here but you may know half the fekkers anyway. It's a magnificent, sneering, surging riot of a record. It's also coruscatingly intelligent.

Rotten's presence slapped almost everything and everyone against the wall. The production – that tremendous racket – was blistering, targeted and intimidatingly inspired. Whatever reservations you may have about the authenticity of any of those involved, it's an almighty record which captures and/or drives a particular moment in a way that makes it special. 'Anarchy' was undeniable – was undeniably an Absolute Monster. It's hard to think of any single popular cultural event that had as much impact, whether you were revolted or stirred towards your own revolt. Reactions bolted (perhaps uniquely?) towards these two poles.

*

So who were the Proper Punk bands? Would that this was an easy one to answer, but it just ain't. It can be a lot of fun – and start a whole load of arguments – based around all of our furies and comforts. Over and above the obvious fabulous/infuriating subjectivity-thing – my phoneys are your fire-starters – I think we have to widen the remit to include bands who are *unthinkable without punk*. If we don't, to be honest, the list is short. (A-and some might argue that this in itself is telling).

We have certain standards: we're not including sheisters in here. As lovers of *what punk and new wave did* we're not about to include clowns like Billy Idol or Sham 69 in any list of Real Punks. In short we'll recklessly concertina our choices to represent the brilliance of the era. This will absolutely mean stretching the definition of punk... and being unashamedly, tribally one-eyed, where it suits my evil porpoises.

Cue the (rock and) roller-coaster. Unashamedly Brit-centric.

The Pistols were punk but The Damned, for example, despite being steeped in it and sounding convincingly *of that moment*, are arguably more of a novelty band than a protest mob: 'New Rose' notwithstanding.[43] (Sham 69 were like this only worse, because of the sustained contact with right-wing support). Stranglers were in a sense at the vanguard but their art-school goth vibe was heavy with virtuoso playing – particularly keyboards – so they, like Wire, like Magazine, like The Jam, were both right in there and not. Like Talking Heads; like Ian Dury. Tremendous and influential (and influenced or kick-started by punk) but not *essentially* punk.

---

[43] Oof. Plenty won't like that!

The Clash were punk, despite the daft fashion-consciousness and Mick Jones's umbilical link to The Bizz. Strummer – the big-hearted one, the mouth, the driving force – was about a bona fide a Punk God as we're going to get. He carried the message, proudly and with commitment. Ramones were punk – despite being American. The Buzzcocks were punky power-chord-pop: but as I loved them and as 'Boredom' sits high in everybody's pantheon they're definitely in.

Lots of folks would say Iggy and the Stooges were essential to punk... and I'm not sure I can be bothered to argue. X-Ray Spex were almost a novelty band, too, but the DIY-and-anti-cool thing gets them in: plus Poly Styrene seemed likable. Mekons we liked for their wit and their clang. The Banshees qualify through Siouxsie's Original Member status and the exhilarating nature of their early sound... but they also get a slap on the wrist for art-school pretentiousness and drift. Alternative TV, Slaughter and the Dogs, Stiff Little Fingers and The Pop Group get high marks for authenticity and The Fall, despite protestations from beyond the grave, must have an honorary membership because the boy Smithy was such a magnificently spiky bastard. And he wrote about 'Bingo Masters' and people coming up to him in the shopping area.

Gang of Four were just about my favourite band throughout most of the period and I liked Cabaret Voltaire. Costello was ever-present and ever-brilliant and Warsaw were punk so the utterly mind-blowing Joy Division are in there. Undertones were a kind of Irish Buzzcocks with a wonderfully anti-heroic frontman so yes. Blondie looked divertingly punk for about ten minutes and produced some wonderful pop so they swan in, albeit controversially, alongside the legitimate kings/queens of feminine rock, Television. Ruts and Chelsea make the grade through making the right kindof sound. Similarly, Au Pairs and Raincoats and Fire Engines projected a certain consciousness – or racket.

As we arc a tad further from the spiky spunkiness, we support the claims of Bunnymen, Teardrop Explodes, Cure, Dexy's Midnight Runners, Human League, B52s, Squeeze and the Postcard Records crew(s) to Associate Punkhood. And lastly for now, we offer the Two Tone crowd – perhaps especially the unsurpassable Specials – that same honour. Many members of most of these bands would note that either something specific – 'Anarchy for the UK?' – or the gear-change in popular music that occurred in '75/6/7 transformed or kick-started their lives.

*

Without quite making it explicit we've conceded, have we not, that we need the term New Wave in here? Nobody in their right mind could argue against the value and the impact of the things that happened in music between about 1976 and 1980. But plenty folks could and do make the argument that punk, or punk-sounding bands only gifted us the leading edge of that. There weren't many quality punk bands: there aren't *that many* great songs or albums to point to.

Unfortunately for us gobshites and psycho-purists there may be some truth in this but if we engage our brains and allow for the obvious, critical mass of energy *directly traceable to punk* then the magnificent near wild heaven that was and is *everything else* hoves into view. Everything from Joy Division and Bunnymen to Cure, Pretenders and Human League. XTC and Depeche Mode. Nick Cave and PJ Harvey. Housemartins. Smiths. Now look at the list of bands over the last couple of pages. Crammed into a handful of years.

Let's circle the wagons of our argument and fire some more political/philosophical rounds. By 1979 Thatcher was a factor in all of this: all-time heroes Jerry Dammers and Terry Hall wee-weed and danced all over her racism, greed and contempt for organized labour. 'Ghost Town' and 'Nelson Mandela' gathered-in everything from the punk/protest/universal betterment departments and smashed the great noises aspiration at the same time. Maybe The Specials became a kind of Apex of Punk, a destination for all of our moral fury and our capacity to dance-with-conscience? I saw them way back when they were still the Coventry Automatics. I don't care if we're blurring boundaries: they remain amongst my Gods of New Wave.

TWELVE – GODS OF NEW WAVE.

JOHN LYDON.

From a blog on bowlingatvincent.com dated Feb 20th 2012. The post was called 'Dumb Questions'. Foolishly, but for 'authenticity', I have changed none of it.

...We are made to feel inadequate. Pressures emerge from all levels of the sky-scraping beast that morphs into (or rises from?) say, the body politic/the fiscal gherkin/the evolved system. Us normal folks are lost or spun or misled by something in the constricting ether; something on the one hand rather rundown and bad-breathlike and on the other awesomely pervasive; powerful.

My instinct is to fight that stuff; to defy and to undermine it. This may mean pushing out beyond the ledge of my core subject expertise – that would be er... sport maybe? – and blowing a raspberry at the notion of received wisdoms elsewhere. Received wisdom often perpetuates myth, right? Is often grounded in smugness; may need the faux-oxygen of privilege or the cover of opaqueness. Perhaps mystery itself may be an outlier in this matrix of conformist gunk? And perhaps, therefore we need an occasional, demystifying blast of... punk?

Punk was wonderful for its moral zeal-with-a-mohican. Punk said – if you were listening – stop preening and start speaking from the heart. Stop twiddling those solo's and tell me something real. It was magnificently articulate and magnificently necessary in that respect. Punk began unpeeling the facades of the worlds of art/music/politics because it seared angrily through; it was a focused mischief blaring wildly out for betterstuff. It may not have paused too long in consideration of the need for nuanced arguments but maybe that counts for urgency rather than in some cool deficiency column. Great punk(s) had no respect, other than that which was earned. Great punks did not understand, so they demanded answers.

John Lydon may have been the only great punk. 'Metal Box' from Public Image Limited remains a staggeringly discomfiting but articulate noise, an appropriate racket from which to launch an onslaught against (capitalist(?)) drudgery—witness the "shallow spread of ordered lawns". Something is being punctured or exposed or better revealed; a kind of hypocrisy, a kind of normalcy; a sad, bad intellectual thinness. There is poetry in these dumb questions. These questions might not have been asked... if we'd have just... behaved.

So though I do despair at how we still fawn before the current gods – for 'growth'/some careering stability/the normalcy of sheepishness – those rib-progglers, those UnCutters, those Occupiers give me hope.

From another blog, on the same site...

I go back to the music, not the construct. 'Careering' or 'Poptones' or 'Rise' rather than the blowtorch that is his 'honesty'.

I go back there because there was – is? – a real subversive majesty to some of that stuff. The Pil appearance on The Old Grey Whistle Test, where Lydon/Wobble/Levene simply disembowel seventies traditions for rawk moosic is in itself sufficient to cut Johnnie Johnnie a lifetime of slack. 'Metal Box' is in itself one of the greatest ever slabs of anything to be committed (and I mean committed) to vinyl. Lydon was the voice of and for this revolution, in which the Pil Army waded in against banality/ capitalism(!)/drudgery and our addiction to sweet melody.

(Here I quoted words from 'Careering').

It's only Johnnie who noticed – who protested – our dumb appeasement to careering like this. He (only) railed against it, with a poet's vision and a lion's heart... and that unholy delivery. OK – maybe only him and (more surreally) Mark E Smith. Late seventies early eighties it was perfectly acceptable to love Cure and JD and Bunnymen and Talking Heads and Television but only he – only Pistols and then particularly Pil – challenged the fraud that is Our Working Lives. He exposed the murderous anti-love at its core; he rose against its cruel unjustness, most magnificently in 'Metal Box'. It's there in 'Poptones', where we – our souls, us the suckers, the minions, the mindlessly seduced – are being murdered in a forest to the soundtrack of vapid music.

(Here I quoted lyrics from 'Poptones').

These two songs, both featured in that OGWT (CAREERING IS HERE – http://www.youtube.com/watch?v=7rtwiMFDWa0) might be the spiritual and political source for everything brilliant from Occupy to Uncut. Or they might just be the greatest (radical?) noises ever recorded by humans. Either way they simply utterly vindicate Lydon and they changed my life.

On every level they are... whatever the next strata up from 'seminal' is. They are fluid and mercurial and bewitching and yet caustic – razor-like. The lyrics are sensational in every way. Levene's guitar is from another, more atmospheric planet. In the same way that Jackson Pollock produced creepily species-enlarging chunks of expressive art, Pil did too. That famous quote (James Blood Ulmer – 'they went right past music') applies. Plus – is it just me? – there is something undeniably beautiful about Lydon's poise, his control of the (quiet?) whirlwind around him. It's inviolably, unsurpassably magnificent music.

Not the case though, that this euphoric peak was flukily ascended in some transcendentally inspired recording session. 'Rise' is palpably also a truly great noise, as were 'Pretty Vacant' and 'God Save the Queen' from the Pistols days. Sure all that is mired in doubts over fashion/puppetry/simply playing The Complex but them were reet powerful toons too.

If a guitar sound can be said to unpeel the corners of the Establishment postcard then the raw, raking racket emerging from The Pistols stacks was it. A personal favourite for me – partly because of that signature mix of moralistic fire and spittliferous attack was 'I Did You No Wrong'. For all that Rotten, Vicious et al were postcards (or cardboard cut-outs) themselves, unsettlingly magic product was the result of the McLaren/Lydon/Kings Road adventure.

So for all the hot air, Lydon has produced. He is bona-fide. Whether this entitles him to be a bore is another matter. Whether it's embarrassing or inspiring to see a worryingly inflated version onstage at Glasto is clearly dependent upon whether you remain either a fan or not. Personally, despite being conversant with the ageism is an nrg debate, I find it (how shall

I say?) unnecessary to go see Pil now. I can still love the old bastard.

Few music icons retain their fire in the way that Lydon appears to have done. But anyway, that back catalogue, those performances, they are enough.

This is/these are my arguments for Johnny Rotten. Believe me I can see how ridiculous some of them are. But as always, the intention is to allow my daft imperfections to reflect something true to the moment.

Familiar with the idea that Pil made 'kraut-rock' and freely admit that listening to 'Metal Box' is maybe not something you might do over breakfast or every day. But am immovable on the idea that songs like 'Poptones' and 'Careering' are amongst the most subversive and revealing noises we've ever slapped down. It's in the words and the manner of the voice. It's in the truly extraordinary bass from Wobble and Keith Levene's inspired and unhinged guitar.

This for me is music of rare *insight* as well as provocation. That intelligence around meaning and purpose was there, I would argue from the beginning – from 'Anarchy for the UK'. As was the drive to make things better.

That first record was arguably about the Music Bizz more than it was about wider politics: about the need to smash up EMI and radio. 'Poptones and 'Careering' are extraordinary railings against blandness and historical unfeeling – there's something unbridled and majestic about their scope. So for his impact and his excoriating artistic reach, Lydon is of course the anti-King of Punk.

STRUMMER/CLASH.

The Clash supported Pistols on that ill-fated 'Anarchy in the UK' tour of 1976. They went on to establish themselves as one of the few bands to be able to make any plausible claim to both greatness and authenticity as an outfit widely identified as punk.

They certainly felt and looked punk when I saw them at Sheffield Top Rank in (I think) 1977. They were raucous and committed, but few of us would have blamed them if – as Strummer threatened to do – they marched off-stage in protest at the hail of phlegm being gobbed at them by auto-punks down at the front. They had a fury and I remember feeling that they could play – perhaps Jones (the muso') in particular). It was an impressive as well as thrilling gig and an early memory of the seediness, edginess and colour of the era. There were outrageous barnets and fishnet stockings; there was leather and booze and more than a little danger.

The early records – singles and E.P.s – were feisty as hell. 'White Riot' may have always seemed a little concerningly ambiguous[44] but the patent love for black

---

[44] Bass-player Paul Simenon's 'Guns of Brixton' always struck me as an embarrassment, in this regard – and because of the transparent and ill-thought-out posing going on around this track. Not making any excuses for the band, but drugs loomed ver-ry large during this time, I believe. Fatally so, for Topper Headon.

music that prompted the career-long crossover(s) into 'white reggae' registered then and now as moments for powerful solidarity rather than cultural appropriation. (I genuinely wonder how they are viewed by those with a different perspective to my own? Particularly now?) 'White Man in Hammersmith Palais' lands with me as one of the greatest moments in rock and roll history: perhaps this is not the case elsewhere?

It was Strummer I loved. Sure he fell right into the imagery but his vocals launched so heartily at us and mostly his Good Man-in-the-Street politics rang true. His vocals on the 101-ers' 'Keys To Your Heart' are a high point in pre-punk action. I believed in Joseph's voice and his scattergun anti-capitalism. 'Career Opportunities' and 'Working for the Clampdown' are tremendous, compelling noises: more overtly political than Rotten, or somehow more specifically targeted than Lydon's material ever appeared.

The Clash produced a slightly mixed bag; I suspect because Jones had different, possibly more 'ambitious' musical needs or was closer to mainstream songwriting traditions than Strummer or the rest of the band. (This is a hunch but I reckon Jones always wanted to be respected in the rock 'n roll firmament in a way that Strummer really didn't[45]). Could be wrong but I'm sticking to that theory. It's why I respected and liked Strummer more: as a kind of heroically honest geezer.

---

[45] Interestingly (or not), I am aware there was a mini-museum thang, featuring Jones's memorabilia, in London during the spring of 2025. It may confirm my suspicion that MJ was drawn to The Bizz and Posterity... or not.

The early punk scene was tight. Guitarist Keith Levene was in The Clash for a period before allegedly tapping up Johnny Rotten about 'doing something together' post-Pistols. (Thank god they did). Bernie Rhodes managed Mick Jones's earlier band (a tad unwisely called London SS) before continuing to steer The Clash forward. Rhodes was an associate of a certain Malcolm McLaren. Strummer was in fact the last key member to join, apparently being persuaded by seeing the Pistols live and realizing this was where it was at. Word is that Levene also played one of Strummer's own songs – yup, the wonderful 101-ers number 'Keys To Your Heart' – back to him, presumably as a mark of respect and to show that this new mob, The Clash, knew what they were about.

On the 29th of August 1976 The Clash and The Buzzcocks opened for The Sex Pistols at Screen on the Green in London. It's not just our friends at Wikipedia who view this as A Moment. Despite music writer Charles Shaar-Murray heavily dissing Strummer and co, it did register as the start (or validation-point) of a movement.

Looking back and reading around, a couple of things strike me. One; that Strummer was very clear about how important the role of The Ramones was, early-doors. (He'd seen them live and was blown away). Two; he was also adamant that his band were 'anti-fascist, anti-violence, anti-racist and we're pro-creative'. The music stayed close to that campaigning ethic, with Strummer being not just a great frontman but a good and deeply conscious fella.

Notes to universe. I have mates who allege that John Graham Mellor was from a pret-ty middle-class background and that Clash signing to CBS early was more of an ending than a beginning. A good deal of the music, however, remained 'political' and relatively explosive – which was presumably why CBS initially refused to give the first album a US release. (This was in effect forced upon them when 'The Clash' – the long-player – sold heavily on import).

The Pistols offered the proverbial short, sharp, shock, being meaningfully active over only a year or so. Clash produced six albums, with the last two being widely regarded as under-achievements either side of the inevitable split. 'The Clash' was the only punk-sounding record, with the following 'Give 'Em Enough Rope' drawing a fair amount of flak for its suspiciously high production-values. (I remember clearly not liking it much: feeling like it was a concession. Rightly or wrongly, blaming Jones).

'London Calling', from 1979, again fleshed-out the range of the band's influences. Rootsy, dubsy, chock-full of reggae and rockabillyfied urgency. You can see why John Langford of The Mekons might say

We loved the Pistols' self-aware nihilism, but we didn't want to be the Pistols... and if The Clash were cartoon-heroic and occasionally a bit silly we still loved them and recognised the risks they were taking.

'London Calling' was a great rock album, by many peoples' estimation, featuring in all manner of Album-of-the-Year polls at a moment that may represent (is this ramping-it up high enough for y'all?) The Absolute Peak of Musical Noises. It may have underlined the framing of the band as punk *rockers* (and thereby challenged some of the safety-pin-wearing crowd) but broadly – broadly – there was still a whole lotta love out there for The Clash. 'Sandinista!', of 1980, extended that sense of musical growth whilst re-centreing the band more obviously on political commentary. The location for that concern – Nicaragua, South/Central America – may have taken us by surprise but the commitment didn't.

For me personally, The Clash were all about Strummer. I'd loved him since 'Keys To Your Heart' for something in that voice. I forgave him the posing and cut the band some slack – a little – around that whole breaking America bullshit. They had, after all, released 'Complete Control' in response to CBS's disputed release of 'Remote Control'; a track the band thought relatively weak. But Strummer was the one I believed in.

MARK E SMITH AND THE FALL.

Mark E Smith was scathing about everything so he might baulk (from beyond) at being offered this honour. Tough. He earned it, for being a one-off and for being edgier than a very edgy thing. He'd hate to be suffocated in cliché as some 'punk-poet'... but of course that's what he was. Dark. Driven. Chronically alcoholic and downright fascistic in his role as frontman. But unquestionably a kind of genius.

Because the music was so angular and so much the deliberate anti-dote to blandness and comfort, he was punk. Because he wrote about daft, working-class things, he was punk. The sound was a kind of colourful chaos – often more colourful and mutable than our conception for punk – but the anarchistic intent locked it into the vibe in a way that extended and re-powered the movement. Plus the fella looked like a punk – maybe, admittedly in the American, 'hopeless layabout' sense of the word.

His delivery was unique; a cross between pub singer and belligerent Northern haranguer-of-innocent-bystanders. The subject matter was wild-but-also-crystalline absurdist nonsense... which he somehow turned into splendid, workaday, story-telling 'fact'. Famously he related to and quoted beat poets, burning their words into an elfish tribute to Ordinary Lives. Fired by the booze, he was relentlessly perverse in song and probably in deed. Similarly perversely, I am proud to be the daft bugger that played 'Hit The North' to National Theatre ac-tors as a way in to my play about football and Thatcherism. (Smith though, would share the Alexei Sayle view of *werkshops*).

Smith auteured his way through 30-plus Fall albums and 60-odd musicians. He married a few of them (boom-boom!) Fabulously he is alleged to have fired a sound engineer for eating a salad. Marc Riley, the musician and Radio DJ *may have been* fired for dancing to a heavy metal record, whilst on tour. To say that Smith was a tetchy soul would be a farting sax of an understatement: he once barked that he got rid of folks to stop things becoming complacent but we can read this as either punk evangelism or bad temper. His cantankerousness was surely exacerbated by his intelligence around the shite-ness of the universe and by drink.

The Fall's first release was 'Bingo-Masters Break Out!' Later titles like 'Hex Induction Hour', 'The Infotainment Scan' and 'Cerebral Caustic' tell you a good deal about their obtuse or abstracted brilliance. There was poetry here and there was an almighty bloody challenge. The fact that it was all so clearly tied-in to Smith's bristling working-class sensibilities made it all the more extraordinary.

John Peel was a lifelong supporter of a band the word cult might have been invented for. Peel, like most of us, would no doubt tolerate and even laugh at the manic maestro's manner and opinions. We might be behind that raging contempt for the Music Bizz and even the *Madchester* Scene – despite him being born in Salford. We might smile at the bare botties in 'I am Curious, Oranj/Orange[46]' and at the bare cheek of his whole wild amalgam of dance, literature and post-punk.

In terms of politics The Fall were an obvious and possibly triumphant expression of The Ordinary breaking out of its box. 'Working-class noise' – therefore 'political' and arguably important – and in those dubious sociological terms, classically punk. Lyrics,

---

[46] A dance/opera/punk-theatre show in which he collaborated with Michael Clark. It is notable and perhaps typical of Mark E Smith that his then wife, Brix, received no credits for her significant contribution to this project.

however, may be wildly ambivalent or expressionistic, but somehow returned, probably gurning, to that weirdo in the pub.

We should not obscure the fact that Smith was a difficult, troubled and even reactionary man. But he was unique; he was prolific; he was sharp as hell and influential. He *did* lead something rare and authentically raw. The music changed, individual songs changed, almost every time they were played live. Fall could be a sort of power-rockabilly or angular electro-dance. I saw The Fall in Grimsby, in the 'Dragnet' era. They made a fabulous, barely-controlled racket.

PAUL WELLER/THE JAM.

Starting this with a late insert. Feb 18th 2025 and Rick Buckler, The Jam's drummer, has died. It makes me very sad. It reminds me how I sprayed a decent but amateurish approximation of The Jam logo onto the wall of our tiddly attic room. Probably in '77. In spidery black paint. I kept my records up there and my Vox AC30 (valves – yup, just like theirs). I was no kind of a drummer but did learn the riffs and chords to 'When You're Young' and 'Eton Rifles' and more. I felt like a god when I cranked up that amp.

The Jam were **everything**, consistently and often electrifyingly delivering in an extended purple patch that may have started after it was accepted or mandated that Paul Weller was the lead songwriter in the band. (Bruce Foxton, ultimately the bass-player, contributed a decent dollop of material over the first two albums but the guitar-player's songs were plainly stronger. Oh – and his dad was the manager).

In '77 they were pitched into punk tours alongside the usual suspects – Clash/Buzzcocks/Slits – and matched or even surpassed them all for sheer energy and levels of performance. They were thrilling live and improved as a band in every respect, after 'In The City' then 'This Is The Modern World' established a platform of authentic and dynamic choons. The influence of Beatles and Kinks certainly loom but The Jam did produce their own wedge of powerful, if quintessentially English music.

Mid or late career, I remember vividly feeling a weird almost nationalistic pride when a noted music mag subtitled a pic of Woking's Finest 'The originals and still the best'. They were right, in a sense. The Jam owned the progressive scene. They were mighty and magbloodynificent just when some of us needed it.

They weren't flawless either politically or in terms of that daft image-consciousness-thing. Clearly they were sartorially-inclined towards Mod-dom from the start but their own, thrashing, youthful dynamism plopped them into the lap of punk, which they used and matured in a way not dissimilar to The Clash. The Jam probably did look great but the sound and the intent was always the thing for me. That whole diversion about which camp they belonged to bored most of us as much as it bored Weller. Juvenile. Irrelevant. Listen to the music.

'In The City' was a stirring beginning. It had force; it had attitude. It was close to punk this, *all-out*, rivetingly based on the anger and disaffection we felt. Weller sang furiously and hacked hard at his Rickenbacker. Bless 'im, despite the inevitable gravitation towards artsy venues and orchestral arrangements, he's still doing some of that in his musical dotage.

The band began as a group of schoolmates doing American rock and roll numbers, before Weller found The Who (and the whole mod lifestyle). This turned them on to Stax and soul covers before the ultimate and iconic three-man line-up of Weller/Buckler/Foxton found themselves in 1976/7. From here-on-in a sort of conscious mod-punk took hold. Like The Clash they signed to a big label early (Polydor)[47] and this may have prompted the growth (or capitulation?) into bigger, rockier sounds closer to the mainstream.

By accident or design The Jam were not controversial. My strong sense was that in the early days they were probably as naïve or ambivalent to politics as most of us, aged 18. Or possibly relatively ill-informed. Some of the material was defiantly anti-establishment but their Proud Englishmen vibe and use of a union jack, stage-side did project a certain conservatism. (Weller later contradicted this and was a supporter of Red Wedge at one time: at the time of writing he has been openly and publicly supporting Kneecap, in their blistering campaign to call out the genocide in Gaza and demand freedoms to protest).

---

[47] It may have been unrealistic to expect or hope that bands that were obviously going to be MAJOR might stick within the wunnerful and wholesome Independent Labels sector. (A phenomenon that may have been Punk's Greatest Triumph). But we did hope for that. In vain, of course.

He liked his poetry, supporting a literary mag of sorts, and name-dropping Shelley, Blake and others as influences and even touchstones throughout his career. (That figures, eh?)

The Modfather became an articulate voice off-stage, perhaps whilst remaining tactically quiet, for the most part, about 'issues'. (I write this then wonder if it's *fair?* Was his profile just a little reduced – and therefore we just heard bit less?) Whatever, we can make the argument that The Jam fell in alongside punk and *did* protest some youthful fury – 'This Is The Modern World', 'Mr Clean', 'The Eton Rifles' – but felt equally comfortable delving into the personal or less stridently observational. In short they were a wonderfully-rounded, contemporary English rock band. *Plus*.[48]

Looking at their discography it's clear that the mighty series of singles – which included worldies like 'Down In The Tube-station At Midnight', 'When You're Young', 'The Eton Rifles' and 'Going Underground' – out-performed the albums. Again like The Clash they produced six studio LPs and probably only two – 'All Mod Cons' and the almost-a-concept album 'Setting Sons' really stand out. But the stream of punchy, relevant, spiky-if-not-punky singles holds it own against almost anything... and was staggeringly commercially successful. Somehow it felt right that the huge following and record sales in the UK were never remotely matched by interest from across the pond.

---

[48] Memory dances in and out. I am suddenly recalling just how powerfully Weller's contempt for the blandness of Ordinary Living affected me. 'Mr Clean' I would never be.

Weller it was who split the group, against the wishes of the other two. On the one hand he may have 'finished at the top' as so many aspire to do but the frontman's need to experiment and develop hurt more widely than just Foxton and Buckler. They had been the greatest band in the world (or pretty damn close) between 1977 and 1980. They represented us spleeny limeys so well. Sadly the unilateral nature of the decision led to decades of bad feeling between band members.

Paul Weller has grown old gracefully and retains a significant following. (It's one of the reasons he's here). The Style Council (immediately post-Jam) never really did it for me – too smooth, too self-consciously orchestrated – but you could see and probably respect that Weller was honourably searching for something. 'My Ever Changing Moods' is some sort of mellow classic, arguably: but plainly a long way from 'In The City'.

There have been significant highlights in his second/third careers and possibly increasing respect for the man's integrity and heart. 'Pebbles On The Beach' and 'Wild Wood' ooze a certain quality but I am most drawn to those days when The Jam plugged in their Vox AC30s – yes, I did buy one – and gave it some.

DEVOTO/SHELLEY/MAGAZINE/ BUZZCOCKS.

This may be a foul calumny to gather in two different geezers and their bands but hey-ho. They share a contribution to one of indie-punk's absolute icons – namely 'Boredom'.

The title; the riff; the words; the posturing, with that irony and street-urchin-mischief. 'Boredom', from the 'Spiral Scratch' EP, of 1976, IS a classic of the period, for everything from the thrash guitar to Devoto's delivery. The mad 'guitar solo' and buddumdedum-ness. The cheeky-chappie banter-poetry. How Devoto looks, on the cover. The laddishness. Is it punk? Yes and no: but it's not fucking Fleetwood Mac.

It was the one record Devoto made with The Buzzcocks, whom he left within a year. (That's some strike-rate, though, eh? One disc and it's Spiral bastardin' Scratch! Beat that baybee).

Howard Devoto (nee Stafford), born Scunthorpe 1952, met Pete Shelley (then McNeish) and Ben Mandelson during college years in and around Bolton. (Yet again) inspired by the Pistols, Devoto and Shelley formed The Buzzcocks in 1976. They are essentially a Manchester band, whatever that means, and made their debut supporting The Sex Pistols in that fair city, in July 1976. Shelley took over singer/frontman duties from Devoto when he skidaddled.

The Buzzcocks released 'Spiral Scratch' on New Hormones, their own independent label. It sounded wonderfully and appropriately DIY and presaged a series of sublime punk-pop singles which retreated into adolescent themes, albeit with a certain Northern wryness. Shelley sounded as wise as he did naïve, on 'What Do I get?', 'Ever Fallen In Love (With Someone You Shouldn't've), 'Everybody's Happy Nowadays'. 'Ever Fallen' was a brilliant, deserved chart hit, reaching number 12 in October 1978.

There was a certain modesty and integrity about what Shelley, Diggle and co were doing. Buzzcocks were thrashing out great choons with a distinctive grungey sound and a crafty, throwaway wit. They were statements about pop, certainly and about love, (mainly), but alive to and aware of *issues* – of sexual politics – largely dealing with things via irony or mischief. You could shuffle to this by the sink but it was never air-head pop, though in a sense it referenced or even used it. Buzzcocks sounded of the moment and they *knew*.

Devoto set up Magazine and continued to put out material with pret-ty astonishing philosophical insight – yaknow, for 'pop music'. Albums were critically well-received but sat proudly apart from Ordinary Rock and the Punk Scene that Devoto had expressed serious misgivings about. (Basically he felt that like everything, it had quickly become predictable and kinda lame). Crucially, he came up with 'Shot By Both Sides' – towering and defiant – and the worldie that is 'Song From Under The Floorboards'. This remains one of the finest, most beautiful and most insightful rock 'n roll lyrics of all time. As always, Devoto didn't so much sing it as inveigle it out there.

My understanding is that I can't quote the lyrics – so be it. They deal with the meaning of life in such a profound and yet casually-generous way I can only urge you to go look, go listen. This guy is being *seriously brilliant* about the state of things – his, ours – because *that's who he is*. In the process he's sending out the message that even daft wee punk songs can carry our most portentous imaginings. You should know this but if you don't....

where have you been? If you don't know that three or four minutes of warbling on vinyl can be stirringly chock-full of top-end Human Expression and Artistic Integrity, where the hell have you been?

The tortuous synth and of course the delivery won't appeal to everyone, by any stretch. But hey, words in songs don't get any better than this. I'm not ruling out getting significant lumps of it tattooed onto my ancient and unappealing body. Maybe that can testify to its utter, captivating genius?

'Floorboards'. (A-and breathe). I may be cheating again. Putting favourites in here, even though they are clear outliers from punk *itself*. I would argue that a) this is my book (nernernaner-ner) and b) punk was about (the pursuit of) truth, integrity and the making of new, real, conscious, contemporary noises. However daft you may think that sounds. Devoto and Shelley are in.

SIOUXSIE AND THE BANSHEES.

I listened to 'Hong Kong Garden' at 9 am of a drab, Feb, Tuesday morning to re-psych myself into this. In 2025 it still registered as a pretty electrifying dose of punk-bling. In 1978, after something of a wait,[49] that iconic riff – which I now know was recorded using a pixiphone then xylophone alongside the fabulous, riveting guitar – was like nothing we'd heard.

---

[49] The Banshees seemed to take an age to get sorted. We were aware of them but when 'The Scream' came out – albums came out, rather than dropped, back then – it did feel thrillingly different and new.

The Banshees started with Siouxsie and bassist Steve Severin falling into the early Pistols entourage. Somebody stuck the label 'Bermondsey Contingent' upon them, which they probably both enjoyed and resented. In a very real sense they were part of the imagery and performance of Original Punk. The two inserted themselves into the 100 Club Punk Festival of September 1976 (headliners, guess who?) when another band dropped out.

In one of the genuinely seminal Punk Moments the scratch band, virtually unrehearsed, screeched and wailed-out a deliberately confrontational version of the Lord's Prayer. For twenty minutes. With Sid Vicious on drums. It was a classic, DIY inflammation that kick-started the Siouxsie legend and launched hundreds, maybe thousands of mad punky teenagers towards 'just doing it'. Pre- Nike.

It's unclear what led to the delay around the inevitable recording contract and establishment of a 'proper band'. Could be that either or both of Siouxsie and Severin *really were* ver-ry clear and determined to hold out for the control they wanted and the people they wanted. That was the whisper. In any event it was almost two years before the Banshees delivered. After signing to Polydor.

The line-up changed significantly during and after that contract was finally completed. John McGeoch (of Magazine) and a certain Robert Smith had spells on guitar and Budgie – a talent of some renown who had been with The Slits at one time – came in on drums.

Over their career, the Banshees put out eleven studio albums. There were multiple changes, with fans and critics alike distinguishing between Banshees Mark 1 and 2, often aligning around specific guitar-players.

We should note in passing that Peter Hook described them as a huge influence on Joy Division, chiefly for the sound. And that figures as notable as PJ Harvey and Thom Yorke cite Siouxsie and co as instrumental in powering them forwards towards performing themselves. Robert Smith is also on record as saying that playing *in* the Banshees made him feel quite differently about music. All this feels BIG and worthy of respect.

I have maybe under-achieved in terms of support for Siouxsie and the Banshees. I loved them briefly and then the interest dipped. I think because it felt, in 1978, when I was young and even dumber (and *at least* as judgmental), that they had shifted ground. The band-leader(s) may have gone exactly where they wanted but 'The Scream' struck many of us as worryingly *slick*, reaching concerningly immediately for a kind of heavily-produced, artsy goth. Some of it still sounded magbloodynificent but I personally suspected another case of The Bizz changing the feel and the sound of things early-doors: for 'strategic reasons'. I may have been wrong.

So I've followed the career of Siouxsie and the Banshees from a sort of respectful distance. Dipping in there occasionally, over the twenty-year span of the band. 'Hong Kong Garden' was extraordinary and striking but it's by no means an exceptional Banshees number. (It just sounds that way). 'Happy House,' for its jangly irony or 'Helter Skelter' for its utter and courageous re-birth of a Beatles record may be. 'Jigsaw Feeling', too. But you choose.

I absolutely accept the status of Siouxsie herself as a full-on feminist icon – even as a kid I think I had some growing appreciation for that. She is a special figure who has engineered a legitimately central position in alternative rock music. She was and is punk in that critical sense of being driven and bold and committed. Her look and her stridency have always been essential to any appreciation of this movement. She is one of the keys.

GANG OF FOUR

Grimsby. 1976-80-odd. Me and my major partner-in-crime looked like the Gang of Four... because they nailed loadsa stuff. They made a tremendous but articulate noise. They were unashamedly political – and of The Left. They were fuelled by anger at the wretched blandness of everything and the patent injustices around money. Plus they had a producer/sound engineer name of Rik Walton. (Hear he's still claiming to be me. *Major wink emoji*).

But seriously, they were tremendous. Andy Gill's guitar was uniquely punky-funky (or something) – but unique. Jon King sang the Marx-influenced lyrics with a studious but compelling diffidence. Their only possible weakness was that they sounded a bit like a student band: and we – from our position of strength (on the dole or in shit jobs) – hated students. But we bought the records and wore the overcoats.

The outstanding debut 'Damaged Goods' launched them into clear red water as probably the most keenly, challengingly and overtly politically-motivated band out there. They had brains. They called-out capitalism – it was up-front and central. They knew who Lot's wife was.[50] There was masses of space inside the music, with audacious, imperious bass. Then Gill would slash through it with his guitar – thrillingly.

Again not uncontroversially, the band signed to EMI. Predictably, this led to 'issues' – like when they walked off the set of 'Top of the Pops' after the Beeb told them they couldn't sing the word 'rubbers', from their single 'At Home He's A Tourist'. Despite industry unease and that whole conspiracy against driven and committed alternative choons, 'Entertainment,' the first Gang of Four album, charted at number 45, in the UK. Why? Because it was brilliant.

The band's career, like many before or since, may have peaked early. Certainly internal disputation played a part in undermining both longevity and legacy (although versions of the band stumbled on, incredibly, into 2019). But their contribution was powerful in an austere, focused kindofaway. We needed folks to protest and they brought that with style and energy and authentic

---

[50] Erm, I didn't. But the fact that they would make that reference smacked of a kind of intelligence and maybe even defiance that was what? Notable.

verve. 'Damaged Goods' and 'Entertainment' remain inviolably important to the punk/post-punk canon.

IAN CURTIS/JOY DIVISION.

I know, I know. We're stretching the elastic, here. But given that Joy Division produced some of the greatest noises ever made by humans – and more zoomed-in to the task in hand here, Warsaw, the pre-JD incarnation were punk – they're in. Live with that.

Active from 1976 but not producing an album until '79, Joy Division remain Big League in terms of their impact. Hard to separate the music from the tragedy of Ian Curtis's suicide and, know what? That may not be necessary. After that terrible event (May 1980 – Curtis was 23) band members could barely believe how stupid they had been not to see the trajectory towards his death in the songs. They probably were stupid, or distracted... but what songs they are!

Curtis wrote the lyrics, capturing most of life's melancholy and existential strife in a way that was both strangely saintly and readily understood or imbibed by Ordinary Joes like you and me. It's not just the obviously beautiful and profound numbers like 'Atmosphere' and 'Love Will Tear Us Apart' that creep into our deep corners. Everywhere you look and listen there's a kind of uniquely penetrative soulfulness.

This may not be very punk or even sound very punk but as a lost boy taking issue with the incomprehensible hurt and injustice in the universe, something about these noises chimed. It even felt good and bold and truthful that soulfulness was not something to be remotely ashamed of – and as a hormonal and necessarily macho-aspirant young bloke Up North (or anywhere else) you really might be. Curtis and JD legitimized that.

It's fascinating and it figured that half the band hated what Martin Hannett did to their music when they first heard 'Unknown Pleasures'. But the contribution of the bloke in the studio was surely one of the most inspired and resonant through the history of popular music? Hannett brought space and grace. He somehow brought the balance between ethereality and transcendental import. Joy Division – unlike Warsaw – sounded massive and yet airy and vulnerable and true. They sounded like royalty *and* the homeless. The production was literally sensational, with Peter Hook's bass high and handsome and the spangly, tricksy stuff shaken over the mix like miniature stars.

Joy Division had been electrifyingly stirring when driven by Sumner's minimal but-also-killer guitar riffs: I'm taking 'Transmission' to my Desert Island on the grounds that its unbeatable swing and swagger and that whole antidote to radio-thing is un-bloody-beatable. But though Hannett shifted their ground away from that guitar/bass/drums shemozzle towards something utterly different through 'Unknown Pleasures' and 'Closer', he magicked-up a natural, spellbinding progression. There are stories that he was unbearable and completely off his head, when in the studio. But Hannett captured this thing for all of us: he may even have built it.

Over two cruelly short years Joy Division crammed into their story an unwise and unfunny dose of Nazi imagery,[51] truly great guitar-based songs and the ecstatic, yet solid fusion of a new music. It was – 'Closer' was – a new register, somehow realised via traditional instruments, arguably unremarkable vocals and the twiddling of knobs. It was, almost shockingly-beautifully, 'Heart and Soul'.

They did this with a semi-detached lead singer who could not ultimately bear his chronic hurt, the mess of his life and his epilepsy. But Curtis did manage to share his troubled poetry with us – enough to offer a wisdom that maybe we don't need to break down. All that opening and offering is *just there*. Joy Division stir us more deeply than almost any other band you could name. On times we may have done it tearfully but we carried their work in our hearts. We really did.

In about 1982 I was walking down Camden Road (Landun) feeling bit sorry for myself. (What we would now probably call depressed). Bit teary because yaknow – the universe – but also that thing of being really tired of worrying about whether I could afford to or justify buying my Very Bestest Mates a pint or two in the pub down the road. (Have had that pathetic fear many times, being a shockingly inadequate capitalist). I walked home… and I know I was singing 'Atmosphere' (guess which bits)

---

[51] …Which the band may have persisted with out of that juvenile spite that sometimes crops up when folks feel misconstrued. 'Bollocks. We're not changing that', maybe?

as I trudged off. Wasn't posing or channeling anything
feeble. Was kinda desolate. Came through.

RAMONES – AMERICANS!

OK. We've already acknowledged the debt some of Our
Lot feel is due to The Ramones, whilst admittedly
unequivocally casually insulting half of North America.
But look. This *is* a tribal thing. This book won't translate
to American. I can't (actually) quite like The Ramones
like I like The Fall. (And I'm not at all sure you
Americans can remotely get The Fall). Your music may
bleed into ours and vice-versa but there are zillions of
abstract or regional behaviours or circumstances that
are part of the making and marking-out of who we are,
that get in the way of equal-footing.

I say this as a perdy non-nationalistic geezer. A geezer
who was embarrassed by The Jam's Union Jacks and
who sits more comfortably in the almost-Welsh category
than the English.[52]

I can be clear that Tom Waits and David Byrne are utter
legends and have genius and I am a fan. They are in NO
WAY less valuable or central to anything. But in a
fashion that I suspect is to do with the exhilarating, DIY
immediacy and smallness of punk – the niche that it's
in – I don't identify with The Ramones or MC5 or New
York Dolls/Johnny Thunders or Iggy Pop. All may have

---

[52] For newbies: lived effectively all of my adult life in West Wales.
Have politico-philosophical difficulties with much of what we might
call the English Legacy.

been key to the emergence or development of the movement. I respect them all. Just don't feel close to them. I'm not gonna itemize or *appreciate* their particular contributions here – apart from Joey/Dee Dee/Johnny and Tommy. Didn't really feel or even hear those other guys. Glad you did and do.

Ramones were kinda deliberately dumb-wonderful in a way I really liked. And, given that they had been around from kinda *before* the beginning – '74/'75 – there was no denying their status as Original Sinners. Plus we understood from the start that they were probs the most obvious manifestation of the 'three chords is plenty' mantra – thereby opening-up music to every Tom, Dick and Dee Dee on the street. Seriously, this *was important*: as important to the de-mystification of popular arts as the usurpation of Proper Portraits by ideas and videos was, in the visual realm. They also had something that was *their own*. The fact that that thing was plainly witty and self-effacing made it fun.

Tempted to lever in the name of Johnny Thunders here, if only because a mate of mine got off a potential speeding charge, when hauled in on the M4. He told the rozzers he 'had no choice but to drive quickly… because of thisss!!' (At which point he turned the CD player back up, to assault the hard shoulder with Johnny Thunders on the rampage). They laughed and said 'fair enough', before sending him on his way.[53]

---

[53] What I fail to mention here is that said full-on rocker in this story might actually have been Johnny *Thunder*, who could also give it some wallop.

Iggy was obviously an inspiration to many, for his subversively anarchistic 'antics'. Plus there are plenty of clanging guitars. I may have been in the Not That Bothered camp... perhaps because I found the druggy mess vibe – the bean-spreading and 'off-it' nudity – more indulgent than funny. Mr Pop, however, has challenged almost everybody and everything for fifty years and more... and like Paul Weller (weirdly?) has gathered integrity points with age.

Look. I'm conclusion-averse. America *may* have started all this. But I wrote that sentence in disappearing ink.

Ooh, hold-up. More Americans!

DAVID BYRNE/TALKING HEADS.

It probably figures that Talking Heads emerged out of a bunch of design students getting their act together, then living in a loft in New York. And the girlfriend of one of them learning bass, to flesh-out the sound. All true enough. But more relevantly, they opened for some dudes calling themselves The Ramones at some club calling itself CBGB's in June 1975 and this is why they are here, with us. Oh – that and they made some astonishing noises – perhaps peaking with the 'Fear Of Music' album four years later, a record which may be in the top handful of human achievements.

Not punk, not quite, maybe not ever, but Talking Heads were shot-through with something of that late Seventies edginess, urgency and zeal. They understood The Mission, towards re-discovery of purpose: they had wit in spades. So they *did fit* – despite being irredeemably artsy and 'off-the-wall'.

Lead singer David Byrne was always the focus, being quirky, long-limbed; a sort of Mad Professor with a sideline in choppy guitar. He was throwing a lot of himself into 'Psycho-killer'. He was visual and conscious and yup, a Creative Force, leading a rich sequence of intelligent imaginings, through airy punk-funk, to music videos, to full-length movies. Brian Eno (no less) came in – of course he did – to produce albums that bled richly into afrobeat and a kind of suss North American World Music.

I saw them live in London during the 'Remain In Light' era. Stiff Little Fingers they were not, what with about thirty people on stage, giving it a percussive, dancey, 'African' dimension.[54]

Talking Heads records are almost without exception fabulous: sharp but dreamy; clever, atmospheric and rhythmic. If this is un-punk then prob'ly it is. But they produced material that felt of its time... or maybe even drove that time forward. I love the story that when David Byrne heard the first Bunnymen album he thought maybe his own band should just give up. 'Crocodiles' was so *something* that they hadn't or couldn't capture.

---

[54] Don't remotely mean this in an anthropologically lazy or negative kindofaway. It was one of the best gigs I've ever been to. I think I remember Adrian Belew squirting out some ridicu-guitar, but I may have been yaknow – a bit bendy.

Chill out, fella. Your Americans were just different in a really good way – your own way. From '77 to mid-Eighties Talking Heads were one of the most refreshing and relevant and downright entertaining bands in the world.

COSTELLO.

Roads are leading us back to Elvis. His contribution to popular music over the last fifty years may outrank anyone else's. Powerfully engaged; ludicrously prolific; both soulful and intelligent. Plus a superb singer. I bought the first record... and plenty of the later ones. I prob'ly thought I was him. There's evidence that I'm not.

We both have zillions of brothers but I'm not even part Liverpool-Irish. Declan is, despite being born in Paddington. He's bit older – six years – and Wikipedia tells me two other things I didn't know about the fella. 1. He hosted a chat show of sorts, called 'Spectacle', where he interviewed Reg Dwight/Lou Reed/Bono and The Police, amongst others and 2. Rather weirdly but in a 'somehow yeh, that makes sense' stylee, 'Veronica' was his biggest hit single in the USA. '*Veronica*'. For me this is like an oblique symbol of how much of America *is*: i.e. clueless. It's good; it's catchy. But Costello has four hundred songs better than that. Let's move on.

We both have goggles, but mine were medium-late arrivals, and are barely necessary for everyday life. Currently (like *as. I. Write*) I'm 'recovering from' surgery on my Du Pruyten's contracture of the pinkie and ring finger of my left hand[55] – the chord-maker not strummer, for both of us – which may spookily parallel the 'stiff lil concrete fingers' the boy MacManus has often talked about. Or not. My hands, at least, can hold a tune in a similar way to himself (himself). Or they'll be able to once I get my fingers back (if I do). The voice is a different matter.

Was it Elton John – I think it was – who singled out Costello as a wonderful singer, back in the day? (It was one of the earlier positive proclamations from within the honeyed monolith that is The Bizz). He certainly and obviously is that. Check out everything from 'Alison' to 'New Lace Sleeves'; 'I Can't Stand Up' to 'Oliver's Army'. Now I can't do *that* – very few of us can. The truth is I wouldn't want to: sing 'properly', I mean. In part, Punk Rebellion. In part because I can't.

Elvis the King was a kind of royalty to us. Despite being broadly anarchistic – and republican! – we were aligned under or behind him. The gobsmacking songs kept on coming; brilliant, sharp, on-message to the anti-Thatcherite anger and suss to the dumb authoritarianism of wider commerce and media. Down the line he would sing about himself as a protest singer (see 'Tokyo Storm Warning'): he was all of that – and therefore in an exclusive and for me, honourable club.

---

[55] I was. Op done Sept or October '24. May refer to this again – confusingly, possibly. State of play has changed during The Writing.

Billy Bragg may have approached his brilliance and that searing conscientiousness, through his own, wide-ranging work: 'Great Leap Forward'; 'New England'; 'Levi Stubb's Tears'. But Elvis Costello was yet more productive; yet more immediately on-the-money around contemporary issues, somehow. (It may be daft to go anywhere near hierarchies but we inevitably do. Respect Bragg for his honourable, career-long protestations. If I place him behind Costello this is *all about* that mysterious stuff that chooses our *individual* favourites and our touchstones. Plus possibly something to do with sounding bit punkier or new-wavier on account of the band set-up). The Attractions were tremendous, noisy and spiky. Bragg of course was essentially a solo artist but I should and do salute him.

'Tramp The Dirt Down', Costello's fierce retort to the death of Thatcher captured completely my own/our own contempt for the woman. It was stunning and stunningly abrasive. 'Shipbuilding' – admittedly a song that Clive Langer and Robert Wyatt have made a huge contribution to – is a very different, yet similarly A-list protest song. As again is 'New Lace Sleeves'. All three – and there are many more – combine that clamour to be better, to call out badness, with brilliant intelligence and wordsmithery.

This fella may have done more to give songwriting a good name than anyone. (Seriously... who gets close? For serious as well as beautiful? I'll wait. These may be inflammatory as well as ridiculous questions but... I'll wait).

Costello engineered himself towards punk to kick-start his career. It may even be that his early image – new-wavey geek-with-specs – was insulting to some. But the discography confirms him as a relentlessly, often inspiringly-conscious bloke who wants to point us to better things. That run of seven early albums from 'My Aim Is True' to 'Imperial Bedroom' knocks spots off nearly everything (or possibly everything) in the history of popular music.

THIRTEEN – THERE IS NO ESCAPE.

Had a brilliant conversation with my 26-year-old son. About music, which he loves deeply. He knows I'm writing this thing and that it's largely about the Power of Music, its capacity to protest and maybe change things; or at least energise us as individuals. When I asked him who might be raging now, he, despite being a ver-ry politically-engaged individual, started by saying that most of his cohort are looking to escape from Trump/Musk/Starmer/Netanyahu or whoever. He hastened to add that there *are* people acting out of conscience, and some of these *are* inspirational, but dance, disco and drugs are biggish because "well. Look at all this shit".

'Twas ever thus, of course. Punk and New Wave felt massive to some of us, but was dwarfed by radio and TV and the charts-driven machine. Maggie and that whole late-Seventies bleakness both necessitated punk *and*, utterly conversely, drove a positively carnal desire for wealth and its accoutrements. Money tends to win. No wonder then, that *numbers-wise*, nobody knew or knows what Howard Devoto was all about.

The universe of 'Love Island' distracts us now[56] in the same way that 'Opportunity Knocks' once did. Some of us might argue that the former is more perniciously unhealthy than the latter. Whatever: the argument that capitalism needs escapism is still alive, yes? We are seduced into our dose of drugs and dancing, to keep the peace. My son would absolutely accept that.

I have some hope because his social clan passionately and openly hates[57] what Trump and Musk are doing, and they can and do make the counter-arguments. (They also slaughter Starmer and Netanyahu but that's maybe a story we won't get into now). *The Consciousness* is there... and I'm sure the exponents of protest are there too, in music and the arts more widely as well as in political campaigning or activism itself. It's just that a) I'm older and feeling further away from any musical movements and b) things may be moving even more alarmingly towards *really concerning* situations.[58]

During the time it's taken to write this book so the feeling has grown that America's headlong descent into vileness and prejudice *will mean* a new generation of activism – across political and cultural fronts – arises.

---

[56] Well. Not me – can neither abide nor watch that shite...

[57] That word again. But it's accurate.... And I don't blame them.

[58] Feb 2025. In this month Trump has talked about Gaza in terms of it being desirable real estate... and Musk made a Nazi salute, during a rally. And the Labour government in the UK has absolutely joined with the performative cruelty scene by posting videos of the forced removal of immigrants. All deeply grim.

(How could that not be the case, given the *extremes*, the brazenness and madness of Trump and Musk?) 2025 could be a very worrying year – a historic year in a bad, bad way.

Foolish to remotely compare how things felt from Year A to F, but the parallels around race and wealth, between Thatcherite Ingerland and Trumpian North America are striking. Thatcher (for us) was an obvious bigot and likely white supremacist: see also Trump and Musk. In both eras there is an extraordinary sense of the rich getting richer – *by design*. That shamelessness, now so epitomized by Trump's cohort of oligarchs and technocrats is both the exercise of increasingly authoritarian power and triumphalist cruelty. Meaning a particular kind of wickedness.

In her own way, Thatcher did the same. Right now it feels like the divisiveness she fostered is being recklessly surpassed by what's happening in America. Trump and Musk really are running wild in a way that feels outright dangerous.

One of the essential differences, era-wise is the emergence of an on-line universe which parachutes the Trump-led discourse into almost every room on the planet. Making his lunacy and deconstructions of the truth feel irresistible. As this, together with the broad submission or even approval of the wider media patently assists the oligarchs and demonizes those they want to target, I imagine Margaret is smarting with a little jealously, from her private bunker in wherever. By the time you good people read this, Elon Musk may no longer be a part of the Trumpian firmament. He has though, been central to the dissembling of the truth and therefore the enabling of the shitstorm. The messaging has been inescapable.

We need to oppose and some are. Masses of young people have smelt the rats. Do they have the guts or the vocabulary to rise against? I hope so. Is it not 'natural' to imagine that one particularly powerful means to object and respond might be to grab a guitar, or do the appropriate or relevant *conscious equivalent*, musically-speaking. (Or is that the post-punk in me, *projecting?*)

Appreciate any ripostes might look and sound very different, now. Music can be made on laptops and phones – perhaps more conveniently than on guitar, bass, drums. (In fact this may be something of a concern. You may *not need* to get together with a gang of impassioned mates. This may dilute the anger, some of which felt kinda communal to us, I think. Or, to be fair, it may focus it).

We were probably relatively privileged white guys in out-of-town North Lincolnshire. But hell we were mad. I wish I could be more specific on what exactly drove us but the picture we're painting here of inadequate or developing youffdom, political rage and energy in the ether is maybe a decent social document for the time. And there really was a moral component in the sense of outrage at the injustices we saw or perceived. Whether admirable or arrogant, that judgement of things was at the core of our fury and our music.

So what now? In urban centres it may be that disadvantage is particularly keenly-drawn or felt. As well as any new generation of garage bands, might the 2025 equivalents for rap contests (or DJs, crews or clubs) be the cutting edge? There is plainly an argument that the next Youth Explosion (or whatever) needs to happen in Georgia and Wisconsin more than it does in Grimsby. But that assumes the kind of perspective that may sit outside experience. Wherever and whatever it looks like, I cannot think of a more important time for popular culture to protest its values.

FOURTEEN – (MAYBE WE NEED SOME) SWEETNESS.

I'm struck – or at least interested – by the idea that somehow my (concerningly tribal?) book about British Punk is lurching towards a response to pan-Western political issues. How come we've starting lumping Trump and America in with (yaknow) Sheffield Top Rank? How do we get from ATV 'How Much Longer' to Musk and the creeping (but global?) fear of fascist resurgence? Because my ether *does feel* like it's either expanded, or been invaded, such that the wildness and foreboding that characterizes US politics right no*w* has spread its pall right over and into us here. It's disturbing – as disturbing as the *actual daily events*.

The unsettling universality of fascistcreep must be a function of the capture of the internet and the media by Musk, Bannon, Trump and Trump-lites like Farage. We see them and we see those who have facilitated their truly foul endeavours. We will return to this.

But sweetness... and escapism... via music.

My son loves his music and loves to dance. He knows and loves a gert big wedge of his dad's music, from Smiths to Talking Heads to Radiohead. He's into the words as much as the choons – gratifyingly so. I have no doubt he is pret-ty conversant, in truth, with a good deal of the important or conscious output from across a range of genres. But his group of mates particularly enjoy festivals/DJs/dancing. I'm repeating but he used the word 'escape' when we opened up our discussion.

Do I have any concerns about this? No. They are young. They need to do young people stuff. They remain engaged individuals. It's not like they're abdicating responsibility for or connection to things: or if they do, they're doing it for x hours, whilst hopefully 'blissing out', or similar. Oh – and yeh, I've been there.

Yes I'm afraid I did look like something out of Joy Division/Bunnymen/Gang of Four, in 1980. Meaning kinda baggy and dark and serious. But I too, had my moments.

Our glorious sweetnesses came from all over, because there was great music pouring out at us. Much of it was punk-influenced (and maybe not what you might call Dance Music) but it was sweet nevertheless. (I'm thinking Undertones, Cure, Postcard Records crew, XTC, Housemartins/Beautiful South, Aztec Camera, bitta Madness, maybe, some Joe Jackson or Teardrop/Julian Cope. Plus many etceteras). Closer to dance music there might be Depeche Mode, Alison Moyet/Yazoo, Hue and Cry, B52s, Human League, Blondie, Tourists/Eurythmics, Rezillos, Penetration and then the Two Tone bands – particularly Specials and Beat.

Could be that because we were reading the New Musical Express, in 1976/7/8 – and by the way, we really should be crediting it with a genuinely significant contribution to the progressive scene – we were both impressively aware and informed. So we knew the influence Stax, Soul and Reggae music had upon many of our bands. Some of us found Stevie Wonder in about 1974. Black music figured in our collections and at parties – from the obvious (Bob Marley, Marvin Gaye, Michael Jackson) to the more obscure Stax or Northern Soul records.

We were classically blokey in the sense that stimulants – chiefly alcohol, and often frightening shedloads of it – were used to loosen the inhibitions, pre-dancing. We did go to parties and did go clubbing but in Grimsby and Cleethorpes in this era things were about as unglamorous and non-conducive to expressivity as you might imagine. Largely, we mooched about looking moody.

The Undertones were a favourite... and I think this was because of their sweetness. Fergal Sharkey has now become a hero for a new generation for his campaigning around waterways but we loved the daft sod for his warble and his triumphant unsuitability for pop-stardom. Skinny and anti-fashion. Fresh from tea with his perfect cousin. Irish.

John Peel, to my understanding, had two loves in his life – or *at least* two. The Fall and The Undertones. I'm with him on both. And it's not just about 'Teenage Kicks', absolute slice of perfection though it is. Their sound – that power-pop rumble – and a whole series of singles established them as much-loved contributors to the scene and the charts. 'Get Over You', 'Jimmy Jimmy', 'My

Perfect Cousin', 'Wednesday Week, 'It's Gonna Happen' are not the only genuinely fine singles from between 1978 and '82. The Undertones proper-delivered.

*

I pause here to acknowledge that a) I will have missed half your faves and b) because I'm wondering where, if at all, I pile the mighty R.E.M into this. Ditto The Stranglers, who were also mighty but will fall through the gaps somewhat because too accomplished to be punk and too dark to be sweet. But seriously good at what they did. Slits may have sounded sweeter but also clinkier and spacier, almost pre-dubbier – so closer to punk coz had some of that left-field challenge-thing going on. ('Cut', The Slits album was tremendous. Much later, I really enjoyed the Viv Albertine book, 'Clothes. Music. Boys'. She counted).

The Smiths are obviously post-punk and plainly Mr Morrissey has made himself persona non wotnots for many, through his comments on race. (Clown, for me, around this… but find it hard to wipe out the memory of and indeed the enjoyment of some great songs).

Costello said something to the effect that the Melancholy One thinks up all the greatest titles in the history of music then forgets to write the songs. Hear that but it's also unfair in the case of 'This Charming Man' and 'Every Day Is Like Sunday', to take a couple of obvious examples. So one finishes up conflicted, does one not?

Bit unsure if any sympathy towards is *actively wrong* of me so repeat: I wouldn't go see Morrissey now.

I met Julian Cope – see 'The Dots Will Not Be Joined' – and there's lots to like in his discography, including standouts like 'Reward', 'Treason' and 'World Shut Your Mouth'. (Aware I should mention Teardrop Explodes here, so am). He was and is a sweet, quirky Englishman. Orange Juice were originally a key part of the Postcard Records mob, from Scotland. Find me a better, dancier couple of choons than 'Rip It Up' and 'I Can't Help Myself'. Or more brilliant scratchy-indie numbers than their early offerings 'Poor Old Soul' and 'Blue Boy'. They are magnificent and they fall into this sweeter-than-punk envelope.

There are many others: I have never sought or claimed to be doing anything exhaustive here. My brain would hurt too much. On.

Is it just too weird or too lazy to finish with a couple of noted-but-mixed outliers to any selection of faves? OK. Well I'm doing it anyway. Psychedelic Furs. Friends love them but I couldn't believe in them (from the first moment) and then never gave them another chance. Killing Joke: 'thrillingly and essentially central', but not to me. Could be wrong about both.

Slaughter and the Dogs kinda hilarious (to me) – coz those bus journeys – but a way of life to some. Mekons probably excellent; didn't hear the albums. Echo and the Bunnymen remain amongst my favourite bands... but where to lever them into all this? Let's call 'Heaven

Up Here' (the album) sweet. It's not the first word that springs to mind, but it's a superb record. And 'Crystal Days' and 'Bring On The Dancing Horses' *are sweet*.

Enough. Enough to suggest that crossing some rubicon from protest to escapism involves whole lotta paddling through whole lotta lurv. Love of sound as well as fury.

FIFTEEN – PSYCHOLOGY OF TEEN RAGE AND THE LINKS TO MUSIC AND PROTEST. A CONVERSATION WITH TWO BRAINY PEOPLE AND ME.

Factoid: I know two guys who grew up through punk and new wave, as I did. (By that I mean it shifted them). I went on to do nothing of import but they both became psychologists; one teaching and researching at university level, the other working within the NHS. They are both top fellas and they are entirely legit in terms of that qualifications malarkey. Here I diabolically imagine a conversation between us, about music, hormones, meaning, drive – everything. I think we do this over Zoom, for practical reasons but have to be clear that this represents energies in my head rather than personal or professional opinions from the other parties. We were too busy to do it: they *could* disagree.

RW (That would be me, then).   OK brothers, here's the thing. I'm gonna kinda Melvyn Bragg my way through an 'interview' with you two intellectual heavyweights.

But we can fart and laff. Astonishingly, however – because we or certainly you can do that thing – we are going to unveil the secrets of the universe. Or at least the ones pertaining to punk... and teendom... or young-peopledom... and the energy or the psychology of the energy around protest. Are you with me on that?

M – I haven't the faintest idea what you're on about! (Lols).

W – Neither have I!

RW – Well thankyou for helping an old mate out with such an auspicious and constructive start. Bollocks to both of you. But hey – a question. What's four times twenty-six? No. I understand that for reasons of credibility and your own, personal safety from my legions of hysterical fans, you want to remain anonymous. But could you please start by confirming that you are indeed in gainful employment in the field of psychology? That you have degrees and stuff? Can we start with you, M?

M – I can confirm that I am not M, and that because of your notorious and wildly hostile fan-base I would like to be known as Herbert 'the knife' MacManiac, for the duration of this interview. But yes I do have qualifications and students and staff who have to nod pleasingly subserviently when they pass me in the corridors of University X, where I am employed.

W – ...As a janitor.

M – Yes! As a janitor.

(There are engagingly daft giggles, before W continues).

W – And I can be happy to confirm that I get paid mainly to lay people down... on couches... in a hospital setting... and pretend to support their psychological and emotional needs.

RW – Good. That's all particularly helpful and erm, validating. The watching universe I have no doubt will be entirely reassured as to the value and legitimacy of our contributions. Right. Question. What is the greatest and most powerful jewel in the musical firmament crown-thing? For you. When did you hear it? What did it mean? Give me three if you have to.

W – Oooo Jesus, I knew you would do this...

*M – This is easy, because like all trained psychologists I can employ separate-out-the-faculties mode. So I am saying 'No More Heroes' The Stranglers. Because I'm hearing it in my head **now**... and because I am in our living-room in 1976 or 7... and you RW are looking at the cover of 'Rip Her To Shreds', in the corner, by the record player.*

RW – Oof. Tremendous. I'm there, baby. W?

W – I'm at a certain ska-pop band's gig. Don't feel like I need to name them or that song, but it was wonderful and upful and yeh, a magic moment, for me. (Shit. Already conscious this is much more of a moment than a song... but). Ok. I could say – with more freedom and more exactitude I could say – 'Boredom'. Buzzcocks; 'Boredom'. Yes.

RW – OK, excellent. I'm going to say 'Transmission' Joy Division and I'm going to say 'Poptones', Pil and I'm going to say 'In The City', The Jam. Because everything. But mainly because unusually, I'm the boss so I get to be greedy.

W – Yup. No issues. Makes me think I should add something Gang of Four or...

M – Banshees. Banshees were just thrilling.

*RW – Right. We know we're onnabout **that time**, here and I want to get into this thing of why... and what this might mean... and how this might be (in heavy speech marks) 'natural' – or not. You are my esteemed guests in the hope that you can shed some light – some professional light on this.*

W – No pressure... and no chance!

RW – Of course. To both. But firstly Intellectual Head on. Some memories or reflections on what might be knowable or elucidated or inferred from what for me is still a fucking fascinatingly massive presence in my life. I.E. punk or punky music. Come on, dig deep. Why is this so big?

M – (Takes deeeeep breath). There's a hundred and two things in play. Things around taste, around hearing and registering noises that thrill us or stimulate us. Particular messaging through sound – maybe sound alone. Then visual stimuli – what are we actually seeing, on the record sleeve or on the telly, maybe? How this tribe **look.** *How I might associate with that. Not all of us but many of us want to be in a gang of some sort. I wonder if we were drawn in to those bands, at that time, mostly by noise or by image – even in music, perhaps weirdly, we have everything draped in images...*

RW – Sure. Thankyou.

W – And maybe fascinatingly or even tragically now everything is so visual and so screen-focused in our lives that possibly, possibly more than ever, we can't **just** *hear. So... we're going to get into everything, here...*

M – Yes we are!

RW – Yes we are and this is good, brothers!

W – Clearly there is or has been something deep and maybe 'primeval' about the hearing of sound. And that can act upon us. And it can be wonderful and mysterious and emotive, or not. But – perhaps this takes us away from our subject – but perhaps now we are so captured by imagery that music has less space?

RW – Wow. That's interesting. And it totally fits with my picture of the music industry as something which suffocates some of us – not to sound too interlekshool or righteous. But you know what I mean? Packaging.

M – Yes I think so. There is a parallel between everything post MTV, all the stuff that has accelerated us into the TikTok and You-tube era and mainstream rock and roll from the sixties, say. We've been corralled and deliberately overtaken or surrounded or seduced by imagery.

W – So maybe we don't just hear anything now? Although maybe we never did?

RW – Wow. That's maybe not something I've thought about, not in that way. But hey: it applies. It's relevant but let's zone back in. Punk obviously had something to say about The Biz – about capitalism and truth, yes? What did it say to you – what did it say most loudly?

M – It said something really encouraging about being free. I don't want to bore you with my personal circumstances but it was definitely an escape from some of that stuff.

RW – OK. But why did punk give you that exit-route? Was there/were there other things that could have offered something similar? Hang on. Go on: why punk?

M – To be honest I'm not sure if I engaged with it as deeply as maybe you did (RW). It was bloody exciting; it was rebellious in certain ways... but we didn't dress up as punks did we, or do the mad barnet thing.

RW – No.

M – *But I suppose despite being semi-detached it somehow registered as something wonderful and new and maybe that thing of owning or being inside something different was big.*

W – *Same for me. Although I think I did get a buzz from the sort of political energy. The being angry about things that were happening. We were young and I'm sure we'll talk more about that but one of the things that still feels powerful is a sort of surge in awareness around issues. It was a kind of protestation, a moment of protest and I'm not saying I remotely understood all that – being politically quite naïve – but I got that 'Anarchy' was about tearing up the music industry, which stank, because it was about image and sales and all that shit.*

RW – *Now yer talkin', bro.*

M – *I definitely understood at some level that it was great and exciting and right that Pistols or Clash or whoever were bawling at US radio bands or EMI, or the fucking industry. That challenge they threw out was exciting...*

RW – *And weirdly but fascinatingly for me, it did have a moral component. Johnny Rotten bawling 'I did ya no-o wrrronngg!' And then three years later calling out blandness and careering as filth – in 'Poptones' and 'Careering.' For me, however su-fucking-perior or self-righteous it sounds, the punk mission to subvert and expose lies and yup immorality, was ee-fucking-normous.*

W – I get more of that now than I did. So probably more stimulated (for want of a better word) by guitar sounds or musical energy than by messages... even though I got some of them.

M – If we come back to messaging and to psychology, which I suspect you (RW) would like us to speculate upon, we have to start with an admission that individuals are so-o different and are triggered in such individual ways that we ain't gonna come up with much in the way of definitive answers, here. Even those of us who have studied or thought deeply about our own histories or experiences. I'm thinking Slaughter and The Damned and the Pistols opened something up for me; something I may not have found elsewhere, because like you (RW) life was ver-ry simple and villagey until about 1976. OK. After that we were going into Grimsby and Cleethorpes and we were coming over all hormonal so things were likely to change.

RW – Yeh. I kinda love that we fell into this vortex-extravaganza-thing where punk was stirred-up with the hormonal frenzy. I think it was kindofa wild gift that touched us. Maybe made us. Are you conscious of that? Or how general or typically powerful the confluence of the raging horn (in us bokes) and Our Music is? As a complete amateur it feels rank obvious that lots of us are massively tied-in to the music of our teens. Is that anything more than a daft hunch... an association of maybe quite comforting ideas?

W – I think it's both general and we were a special case... because of that moment. I'm distantly aware of *research around puberty or hormonal development and susceptibility to influences. But to be honest we're in sketchy territory here, because well, how do you measure it? If Subject A says he did this or that – murdered the pope or became an accountant – **because** the Ramones put out 'Sheena Is', how do we appreciate the amount of truth in that disclosure?*

M – Yes. Indeed. There is always this or some degree of unknowability in testimonies so we – as professionals or amateurs – are making judgements – or speculating. We have to build up a picture; know the contexts. It's likely that you (RW) got angry and inspired (or whatever) because the messages were good (in every sense) and exciting… and because in that corny-old phrase they 'spoke to you' at the right moment.

RW – Yeh I totally get that. I'm kinda grateful for the accident-of-birth-thing in play here, in my/our lives.

W – So am I.

RW – So hang on. Can we say anything about that really profound shit around when we really learn or become our selves? I mean in intellectual/behavioural terms I suppose, rather than just behavioural terms. So, when do we start to appreciate what we might term moral dilemmas, as opposed to what's right or wrong in that juvenile way? Does that make sense? When do most of us start being able to make political arguments… and is that in any sense linked to physical development?

M – This is hard – or hard to specify – again because of all that Individual Human-In-An-Individual-Life thang. Context. Lots of stuff is learned astonishingly young – and I don't just mean the 'don't stick your head in the fire' stuff. Rights and wrongs. But schooling, both at home and in institutions, is so diverse and so fickle in terms of power and quality that we keep having to return the question with a 'hang on, now… what's the context?'

W – Yes. I think we can safely say that it figures entirely that we are particularly ripe for being swept up in causes (again for want of a better phrase) when we are in our teens. Most of us have just started to recognize or turn over political or philosophical questions. Most of us are becoming more active participants in the universe, in a way.

M – Yes. We're becoming adults.

W – So this time has a particular power or energy of its own.

RW – So no wonder I went ballistic when Joe Strummer gives it some – *sings! Inna Strummer style* – 'Career Opportunities, the ones that never knock!'

Ok. Did we have particular moments that we can remember or separate-out now, when our souls were fu-cking stirred by a message within a song? I suppose we're almost back to question one, here.

W – The Jam were just fantastic at one stage. They scooted – or scootered, lols – past punk pretty quick, but 'Going Underground'; I remember seeing that on telly. Might even have been on Top of the Flops.

RW – Yeh, think it was. Remember The Jam became massive. I remember this so clearly; it was HUGE.

W – Yeh. Weller was looking very cool and yet it was still really spiky and the whole idea of subverting, going underground, even when maybe I knew Jam weren't that political. To see that, and really dig the music, was tremendous.

*RW – Agree completely. And it reminds me I gave away a really precious copy of 'When You're Young' to a Canadian soul-sister as a farewell gift, I think. And, arse that I am, wrote **all the lyrics** down on the blank sleeve. Could do it now. It spoke for me so-o completely. I think I felt a weird kind of nationalistic pride because they were so brilliant. Even though I was already well-suspicious of the stage-side Union Jacks bollocks. They were godlike for a period – that series of singles, in particular.*

W – 'Tube Station'. 'Eton Rifles' was maybe quite late… but as you say, massive.

M – I'm not just saying this for 'balance', chaps but The Slits were pretty spectacular. 'Cut' is phenomenal – still listen to it. 'Typical Girls' is so smart…

RW – Oh yes. Did you see Raincoats with me, in Grimbo? In about 1742?

M – Ooh yeh. And The Fall. Raincoats battling against crap sound...

RW – And the Fall battling each other! Actually I'm not sure they did, that night. Brancombe Street, was it? Something like that. Different night to The Raincoats? Just a brilliant, angular racket. Smithy doing that edgy weirdo thing. What a geezer, though!

M – Look anyone who comes up with those titles, never mind the music, is a god for me. Especially if he's shouting 'eat this grenade' at all and sundry.

RW – Too right. But ok. I want to batter you into submission and draw something medium-definitive out about the relative power of punk in our lives... and maybe in musical history. How big was it for us personally and where does it sit in musical-historical terms?

W – I do wonder about this. And there is a link to not just deeply personal reckonings with our own levels of confidence and image, but to external stuff – to the National Front... to the miners... to Thatcher. All that stuff that we're feeling again now, about the polarization of things.

M – The anger.

W – Yes, the anger. We're gonna want to quote Pil here aren't we but I think it's fair to describe the musical-political moment as unique – whilst acknowledging that they all are, in a way, right? And that we probably do identify – HU-UUGE WORD, by the way, one which I don't use lightly... we all identify with some quality and energy in that music.

RW – Yeh. And I think quality in both senses, or all senses because the music, the noise plainly had an edge but was also undeniably godlike and bloody marvellous. Maaaybe particularly the marginally post-punk 1979 era.

W – Yes. Unbelievable. Nearly everybody hits a peak at the same time: Joy Division. Bunnymen. Jam. Clash. Gang of Four. Talking Heads. There's no question that people are feeding off each other. I think I grew, in that period.

M – And me!

RW – I think I was completely defined by that period. But come on; you're the professionals. What was it or why was it so 'developmental'- is that a word you would use? (I would as a coach). Why so goddam powerful, Mississippi?

W – You've got external events which you now recognize – you're motivated by them. You have a need and a capacity to express frustrations or maybe just energies within yourself – your growing self. Lydon or Siouxsie or somebody is lighting a fuse.

M – You're ripe for it. In my case as a young bloke I was excited by stuff I probably didn't understand – or need to. I just felt unbelievably drawn. I started jumping on coaches then driving to gigs because it did feel thrilling and... there's no doubt that part of me loved being in that tribe and having reasons to get up, and do things, and maaaybe 'belong'... but I was also alone, through quite a lot of that – or not seeking to 'meet up with a gang of mates'. It was possibly, in a sense, more personal than that. Or more intimate.

RW – Because although we knew people who went, it wasn't like being in a team; we didn't *really* dress as punks – more like kinda casual Supporters of The New Wave. I may have thought I was in JD or Bunnymen or Gang of Four at one stage but I know what you mean. I think it was a deeply individual experience.

W – Maybe because music is – or can be. Yes you're in the crowd. But maybe, as per all the research about babies dancing or responding to music in the womb, you're also able to sort of revel in this personal capture. Which is wonderfully mysterious, perhaps? I certainly recognize that.

M – I suppose we have to acknowledge the difference between listening alone or with a couple of mates, in your living-room and the much edgier, bigger, more loaded experience of travelling to a gig.

RW – Yes. Of course.

M – Gigs are different; maybe, because there was some real danger, right, because of all the battling and the dodgy locations and the physical experience was different – all that fecking noise! – there was something more highly-coloured or in some senses impactful about gigs. Or maybe not?

W – Yeh they're just incredibly different experiences. Gigs as you say more physical in some ways and private listening quieter but maybe not necessarily any less emotive.

RW – And when did headphones become a thing? I don't ever remember listening to music through headphones – I barely do it now, interestingly or not.

M – True. We weren't listening through headphones, I don't think. Not then.

W – No we weren't... and I think there's a mega-thesis on this. The changing universe or the Inner Universe of the 'Phones Generations.

RW – Yeh. There's lots of 'inner' shit we could do a goddam podcast series on. But no – NO-O!! Not the Murderous Psycho-shit of the Modern Youth! Sub-titled Desperately Seeking a Diagnosis. No-o!!

W – Ooof. No. Dangerous territory.

M – Yes. Scary. With or without the music.

RW – OK. So in my capacity as Omnipotent Geezer with a Plane to Catch, I'm going to point us towards the endzone, or invite both of you fine, fine gentlemen to try to round this baby off. By saying something that grapples with this personal love – let's call it that, eh? – of punk – let's call it that, eh? – and the actual, knowable psychological processes. In order to try to make sense or appreciate its power in our lives and maybe in the historical context. Can we do that, brothers?

W – No pressure.

RW – Deep breath and go, M.

M – Phew. Ok. Firstly, an unhelpful truth. There may be no knowable psychological processes.

RW – Lols and cheers! But accepted.

M – OK we loved and were into music, pre-1976, but we recognized a change. There was a change. I think for me the increase in energy and sheer noise and fury in the music that I came to listen to, was I think instrumental. So there's maybe something visceral in there. The actual sound signified a difference and maybe some sort of revolt that 'chimed with me', in the modern phrase. I cannot be sure how or to what degree I identified with this concept of revolt, or whether opposing something or somebody – normal family life? Who knows what? – was key, or was motivational. I did, pretty deeply and obsessively escape into something, and followed a particular band around. They became mates, of a sort, so I guess we can take it as read that I both idolized them and then became close in to their tribe. Probably that thing of separating myself from something, and maybe being notable or even sexy *because of that striking out, was in play. In terms of the music I think I would say that whatever psychological insights may be drawn, whatever 'truths' or processes we might suspect, the music of this period was fucking electrifyingly inspirational and yes: life-changing.*

RW – A-men, brother. Beat that, W, you mealy-mouthed metherfekker.

W – Thankyou and well said and I agree and indeed identify with a whole lot of that. But ok. Yeh. I'm suspecting that if not political then weirdly philosophical things were as you say 'in play' for me. Or to a greater degree. Yes I loved and was thrilled by Banshees guitar sound or Clash guitar sound but without being as close to those political meanings as RW was, the anti-establishmentarianism of punk did motivate me. Broadly or in an abstract kindofaway, maybe – I got a bit of a tingle on listening to Gang of Four because they were in-your-face political in a way that was completely new – or felt it. So The Messaging was influential. We maybe haven't said much about hormonal stuff or adolescence or developmental phases but look, for me, getting horny and boozy is inextricably linked to this... and I think likely to be a bi-ig part of the process for most young people. The hormones are driving sex and also driving awareness and direction: new ideas or new and building understandings.

I'm kinda fascinated by how anger in people – anger at the universe, anger around politics, largely – builds or ebbs away – or stays. I'm feeling pretty 'conscious', still.

I can sense that RW got angry and has stayed that way, or got angrier!

RW – I have. Probably. Can't help it. Punk legacy. Plus family tragedy.

M – Yes. Fair enough. Huge.

*W – What I'm still battling with is the longtime music-lover's appreciation and overview of protest or challenge – from Civil Rights to whatever – with or against the idea or value of punk. On the one hand this hierarchy is completely spurious – we can't measure it, it doesn't matter – and on the other it feels so important to us that we want or need to locate the music that speaks for us high up in some mad pantheon. So maybe what I would say is that **personally**, I think punk and new wave changed my world... and made me more conscious... and made me, maybe over time, consider the things, the life-choices I'd be prepared to make... and therefore it was massive. Punk and new wave made it impossible not to be anti-racist. Made it impossible not to be in some way anti-capitalist or anti-banker or anti greed, or anti-Tory. **And** the actual music, the extended bundle of punk-influenced music, from about 76 to 1980-whatever, was spectacular. If your book, Mr W, is an ode to the greatest period of popular music ever-ever (which I think you've said it is) then I agree. As a geezer and as an allegedly practicing psychologist. In that respect we were blessed.*

SIXTEEN – PERSPECTIVE – HAH – THE PLACE OF PUNK IN TERMS OF OTHER GREAT MOVEMENTS OR MOMENTS OF PROTEST.

Not sure I set out to do it but my wonderful, personal, transformational experience of punk energy and the idea that music itself can change things apparently beyond its reach have become intertwined. And the more I've thought about the particularly rich and what we might now call developmental periods of my life the more obvious it's become that anger and conscience *sparked via music* have come to guide or define who I am.

This book is much more an ode to that fabulous power – to affect individuals, culture more widely and even politics itself – than some narcissistic tribute to Yours F Truly. And the three books in my #lolsobiography are autobiographical because I want to be able to tell truths that I know to be valid, not because of Great Things your humble scribe has achieved or been involved with. *These things* I experienced (and I hope you did too). You can take them (and these books) as seriously as you like: for me they are powerful and true: but I could be wrong.

Music can describe, reflect, light up or emphatically nobble our lives. Very often it does capture the times themselves – the times in which we grew. Of course relating this theory to punk or new wave may seem thin to those who weren't there or those who just don't get shifted by choons in the way some of us have been. But – does this go without saying? – despite ploughing this wild furrow somewhat manically, I'm absolutely hoping that you lot will be dropping your own wee seedlets-of-lurv into it. Surely you *get this?* Surely you have your own songs and moments; words etched over your heart? Tunes that carry you.

Welcome to the club. Whilst I will maintain that '76-82 was massive, not just for my gang of mates but in terms of influencing zillions of lives, I am clear your own vibe is just as valid. Tell me all about it. Your turn will come – make it happen.

*

So this may all be an indulgence. I could be deluded, could be wrong. We're bound to hype-up the things around us when our hormones were hyper-active. Things are or were more highly-coloured when we were young. That perspective is always gonna out-biff real perspective: and I'm fine with that. 'Our music' is always gonna be the best.

Chewing this over with a mate and he offers the thought that maybe Mozart was punk: he certainly set out to provoke The Toffs. My understanding is that the great man had a love-hate relationship with his audience and that the work, beautiful and godlike though it might be, was on occasion(s) specifically driven by conscience and by anger. He was also something of a rebel entrepreneur, hosting his own gigs to make those symphonic but socio-political statements. (Yo, Malcolm McLaren; eat shit!)

No doubt there are other moments in the history of classical music where stories are told in order to bring issues to the fore – duh, of course there are! I'm just not the man to name or describe them, without feeling like a fraud. But I do know new wave.

Spinning forwards, it seems obvious that popular music was intrinsic to the cause of the Civil Rights campaigns of the US. (I recently watched some extraordinary footage of Nina Simone at her fierce, magnificent best. It was a revelation. More on this momentarily). Blues itself may be a resistance movement that dwarfs punk in scale and richness. Some would argue that the folk scene of the Sixties was as hearty and conscious as any period.

Zooming out geographically, of course there are spectacular and seminal indigenous protest songs from the Arab Spring and from Latin-American bands raging about murder, corruption, Western hubris, drugs or *whatever feels most relevant or most obscene* to them. Go find. I found the 'Rolling Stone 100 Best

Protest Songs Of All Time', late-on in the writing of this book. Found it interesting... and a challenge. Not that I'm entirely shifting from my advocacy for punk – no, sir. But a(n admittedly imperfect) 'world perspective', over a century of angry music... well why wouldn't that proffer a question or two?

Nina Simone's 'Mississippi Goddamn' is in there at number 7. (Necessary intrusion from an impatient universe: I bet you wanna know who tops it? Sam Cooke; 'A Change Is Gonna Come, from '64). But let's stick with Nina.

She pronounced herself 'skeptical' of protest music out of concern that it can over-simplify and reduce things of reckoning and complexity. This was before the murder of four black children in the infamous Alabama church bombing and the assassination of activist Medgar Evers, both in 1963. I guess she just got so mad she flew into the writing of one of the most poignant and potent songs of any time. 'Mississippi Goddamn' first appeared on a live album and guess what? It was banned for a period, in some southern states.

Simone also covered the Billie Holliday classic 'Strange Fruit' and in 'Backlash Blues' and 'I Wish I Knew What It Was To Be Free' she railed brilliantly and with passion against the patent, rancid injustice of the time.

Can't wait any longer. *Who, in the time of Musk and Trump, will carry that torch?* This feels like a moment not just for Angels of Protest but for massive, concerted resistance – yes, perhaps led by artists and musicians.

I depart from my (ahem) area of specialism to major on Nina for several reasons. She was radical – she told Martin Luther-King she could not be non-violent. She had a real, sensational power and talked of having no choice but to respond to the evil of the time. Simone's voice and piano are rare, rare things. And she has produced some of the greatest music that's ever graced this planet.

*

In that '100 Best' we find Woody Guthrie – more than once, from memory – but at no. 11 with 'This Land Is Your Land'. We find a reminder that Tracy Chapman's smooth-but-eloquent 'Fast Cars' is deliciously spiky. We remember – maybe with mixed feelings?[59] – one of the superstar protests, in 'Sun City, by Artists Against Apartheid. We get a nudge towards checking out Beyoncé at the Superbowl (2016, she's done more than one!) with her black sisters wearing deliberately provocative Black Power berets and leather military-chic, performing 'Freedom' and thereby making a HUGE POLITICAL STATEMENT IN FRONT OF HALF THE WORLD. (Didn't see it live: am just about to re-visit).[60]

Closer to (my) home there is one of the most upful protest songs ever committed to vinyl – Specials AKA

---

[59] I say 'mixed' coz obviously that whole charity-campaigning thing is bit muddied by the career-positioning thing, yes?

[60] Definite WOW moment. She is a MASSIVE STAR. Whatever you think of Beyoncé, this was a huge, prime-time inflammation.

'Free Nelson Mandela' from 1984. I played it to a theatre group in the hotel bar I was running in West Wales. Resident and rehearsing at our place, they insisted on hearing it at the end of every working day, to fire them up whilst bashing out their own inspiring art.

Number 2 on that Rolling Stone chart is 'Fight The Power' from Public Enemy, a raw and in-your-face revisitation to the Isley Brother's record of 1975. Recorded for Spike Lee's movie 'Do The Right Thing', it may owe its high position in that chart to the exposure around that, as well as its punk-rap brazenness and defiance. It's noteworthy (and I take no issue with this *whatsoever*) that all five of the chart-toppers are by people of colour protesting injustice. Suggesting again how vital a force music can be in offering an outlet, a voice that can really register.

Bob Dylan was at no. 6 with 'Masters of War'. Interestingly – or not – the descriptive blurb alongside makes a link between folk and punk. This book again notes to the universe that profound tradition for conscious stories which is so characteristic of folk music... and, yaknow, folks like us.

Remember Helen Reddy? Just about? Me too. She may be offended by the label 'Australian soft-rocker' but consoled by the knowledge that her 'I am Woman' of 1971 became a feminist icon that bounced down the years. (It's at 73 in the chart). It kinda bounced into my lap because (I'm pret-ty certain I have this right) the England and Wales Cricket Board used the 2013 Katy Perry song 'Roar' – which uses Reddy's refrain – to back some promo stuff I played in schools. (I was, some of you will know, a Community Cricket Coach for many years. Am now just a Pathway Cricket Coach). In this way, Reddy's rally may still be roaring.

The Top 100 of anything is usually reductive garbage; we know this. I take significant umbrage with the fact that 'Guns of Brixton' – one of The Clash's worst songs – is in the Rolling Stone collection, at no. 56. Cobblers. Especially when I'm seeing nothing of Elvis Costello. Not going to go scouring the whole thing again but not seeing 'Ghost Town' (but X-ray Spex are in there) and no 'Eton Rifles' but 'Fascist Groove Thang' gets the nod. Ah well; subjectivity, eh?

Punk-influenced music was and is massive in the lives of many of us. It was populist, in theory and in practice, in a good way. Perhaps most satisfyingly, the advent of Independent Record Labels, or more exactly their *proliferation*, based and inspired around new wave music, was central to making the movement – and that whole ethos around DIY – work.

Real People could make records. To some extent the capitalist universe was bypassed. Yes the treadmill was still grinding and bands were still (diabolically in my view) talking about 'cracking America', but the Problem of Scale – i.e. specifically aiming to make records that would be played across American radio was suddenly drenched in righteous spittle. Tiddly, 'cottage-industry' Independent Labels were pumping out real and relevant music, close to home. That was important. No: it was fucking maaarvellous.

Or'nary 'Erberts could get up and do stuff. Me; you; Fergal Sharkey; Mark E Smith. They could record it, too, and access to new technologies would only increase, thereby (theoretically at least) multiplying the opportunities. New and often more personal or political messages could be sent out from voices previously unheard.

This was the Great Demystification. The offering. You no longer had to be 'musical', or ambitious, or signed to a major. You could go from your bedroom, thrashing three angry chords, to a local boozer or small independent venue. Fair enough, this must have led to some bad art. But it gave us The Buzzcocks and The Jam.

Values were re-set. The power of honest story-telling was re-energised. Truth stood in the doorway. Everyone was welcomed in.

There were a million fakers, from Billy Idol to New Romantics down the line but something *did change*. The mighty and sensational music produced late Seventies/early Eighties – Joy Division, Echo and the Bunnymen, Talking Heads and the soon-come Two Tone era – could not have happened without the spark, the release, the (yes!) moral judgement and the *idealism* of punk.

SEVENTEEN – HANG ON. HOW'S YOUR HAND, SON?

Timelines, publishing practicalities and my (ahem) Du Pruyten's 'recovery program' all get in the way of a definitive and up-to-date look at how things are, vis-à-vis my potential for a late-flowering rock and roll career. Maybe if I *just keep writing*, eventually those crippled fingers will spring remarkably into life, and I can produce an updated product, bringing welcome news. But on Fri 5th May 2025 I have to report that things aren't looking good.

Hospital physio has kinda fizzled out, after firstly the practitioner then the victim had to miss sessions over Easter. I'm still working at it – massaging with oil, squidging a softish but springy ball – but there's no denying that progress over the months has been minimal. I won't give up on this (and I am by nature an active fella) but it's possible that short of playing left-handed, my guitar options approach the Less Than Zero zone. (And yes this *is*, in the vernacular, gutting). So let's have a wee dose of the hopefully restoratively sentimental.

*

Some of the story about how I got hold of the two guitars
I still own is in the previous books. So I'm barely going
there. (But). The Ibanez acoustic was bought in fabulous
innocence at a music shop in Grimsby. 90 quid, from
memory, which was a decent lump of money in (about)
1978. My old man had shockingly died young and mum
really did do that thing where she said 'he wanted you to
have one': both wonderfully poignant and a little strange,
given the absence of music from my father's imprint[61]. I
got the guitar and a hard case, having sheepishly played it
very briefly. I knew nothing about anything back then,
but fluked it. It's a beautiful, woody weapon.

The other geetar adventure is somehow harder to grasp.
Know I went to Manchester; think it was on National
Express buses or equivalent. Flew solo. Ah: but
confliction. Cannot be sure which axe was purchased
first – though the strong suspicion is it was the acoustic.
(Why would I not be clear about that? That because
these things are so-o heavily loaded with sentiment or –
call it what it is – grief? Dunno). Anyway, I got to
Manchester with £120, which I had probably earned
doing a factory job, burning the proverbial hole. There
was a destiny/determination overlap in play. I was as
sure as hell gonna buy a guitar.

On that bus I must have been thinking about what sort
of weapon I'd be investing in. Don't think I've ever been
about *A Look* but I did want an axe that made me feel
(and o-kaay, look) like a part of the Brotherhood of

---

[61] Acksherly no. Dad left behind some Satchmo 45s, some Ella
Fitzgerald and an album or two of Western film music, so he had
great taste. But just didn't *feel* musical.

Dark Subversives I'd pretty comprehensively committed to. This would mean looking at good secondhand guitars, almost certainly. Fine; but I had no idea what would be available or within financial range.

Music was so massive I must have been thinking about being in or setting up a band: but hard to be clear about *who with*. (The Boys Most Likely To were buggering off to college). I know I was fearless enough but it would have to be with the right people: uncompromising bastards like me. The Message and the intensity would have to be central and in-yer-face and I suppose this did infer a particular set or support-cast of 'images' – of clobber.

Weller had made that Rickenbacker look his own but that might be tempting, if unlikely, on the dinaros front. Not sure of timings again but Wakeling at The Beat had that groovy-but-weird thing that may have been the same as Ian Curtis's. Sharp, elliptical(?) shape. I quite liked the Gretsch/big electric-acoustic thang that the Stray Cats strutted with and Edwyn Collins may have sported – possibly alongside Ibanez/Yamaha? (Whatever; big-bodied, with f-holes).

Andy Summers, from The Police, who were obviously never really part of our punkstergang but put out some choons, had Arias that might be at the edge of contention. Telecasters were possible but Strats unlikely. Gibsons, Les Pauls especially, were too seventies or too boringly God Bless America (or something). I bought a Gibson Les Paul copy, in sunburst: still have it.

It was functional; in fact my mate Jay Booth, a Proper Musician told me it had 'fantastic sustain' but I never liked it and barely knew why I bought it. That burning hole, presumably. I may have comforted myself with the fact that the lad from Undertones had a red Gibson which he played on several great post-punk singles including the magbloodynificent 'Teenage Kicks'. So it would be passable if the moment came. It never did.

But from guitars to, yaknow, *songs*. Because it's almost relevant and also there's something that's kinda grated for forty years.

Is it just me who falls into learning *part of a song*, like *endlessly?* Or gets past that stage but then still almost never nails the whole lump of it *by rote*, to the end, solidly? So if (even) your mates or family asked you to 'play us something' you'd probably be left flailing, despite being decent enough to impress most non-muso's with your (actually pretty undeniable and functional) musicality. You can, or *could* knock out thirty seconds-worth of something genuinely tasty... but then forget the chord sequence, even when it doesn't change – and most don't.

That's me, all over. Have a good ear. Learnt chords and/ or killer riffs easier than most, I think, but then unable to stick with them to the glorious or bitter end... two minutes thirty seconds down the line.

*

Ach. Another chronological lurch. Thinking back further, I did get a cheap electric guitar for Christmas, when I was maybe fourteen/fifteen. Had forgotten that. Think that was the year we got Rajni the wildcat kitten, who rocketed up the curtains and then bolted out (and presumably back to the farm from whence she came), never to be seen or heard of again. Dad had sorted this; a kitten from a farm near Caistor in the mid-Lincs Wolds. He was teaching at the local Primary and 'knew people'. Nice idea; shite execution. Rajni was a momentarily thrilling package but on the untamed, possibly manic side of feral.

That axe was one of those crude catalogue-types: a strat (ahem) copy, in red-maroon with black flames, I think. Secondhand, so probably not *actually* levered out of a catalogue. Strings set about four foot six above the fret-board – so hard to play. Later I also got a wee practice amp, possibly a 9 watt battery job[62], which gave out a medium-punchy and satisfyingly raw sound entirely appropriate for the Clash numbers and Buzzcocks riffs I soon moved onto.

The noise was a bit fuzz-pedalesque in a way that worked. I remember me and Mark Cheeseman wrote a daft-punk indie G-A-D thang which had a line about 'the poems of E J Thribb' in it. (It may have finished "So. Farewell. Song!") Recall a certain level of irony – Mark sang bit like John Otway – as yours truly strummed or chopped or blocked the chords. Bit Stiff Little Fingers or Wire-stylee.

Mark's eldest brother John was a fantastic guitar-player – or seemed that way to an impressionable teen. There was a story that he'd turned down a slot in the

---

[62] Would that be right? Biggish, cuboid battery?

Buzzcocks and it may be true. A) Because he was plenty good enough and b) because he was older than us and may have viewed 'the punk thing' as something of a passing irritation.

However it was John who later showed me how to play a version of 'Poptones' (PiL), which is and was kinda tricksy. Their axeman Keith Levene was a proper, distinctive talent: the riff (if that's what it is) falls over itself as it 'drive, drive dri-ives' through the trees. I'm aware of the seminal Metal Box album being described and dismissed as a sort of kraut prog rock. Hear that but not having it. 'Metal Box' is one of the great, challenging noises made by humans.[63] Levene and Wobble were outrageous and rich contributors to that incredible album.

John C was also responsible for putting me in front of a simple four-track recording-thingamajig: this was probably 1979. He played around with a Talking Heads riff. I was well-naïve but it was fairly intoxicating. It remains the only occasion in which I have experienced anything approximating a studio. Know that these things have changed, that nowadays you don't need anything more than a laptop, potentially, but still hope to have some kind of adventure in or with recording clobber. Yaknow: 'tape' something properly.

---

[63] Prone to hyperbole? Moi?

EIGHTEEN – POLITICS NOW: THE NEED FOR A SECOND COMING.

Sure in some ways I'd like to write a quiet-but-thrillingly-dispassionate book which was clever and mature and academically strong enough to account for the music of my chosen age. But bollocks. Given who I am and how I feel this route would be a nonsense – more of a nonsense than what we have. I'm a) grateful and b) hopeful that those of you who have made it this far understand that a sort of cool, academic approach would be both beyond me and wildly emasculating of the power and feeling of the moment of punk... and the moment of now. It would be a pack of brilliant lies. I'm offering my lurid truth.

I can't and won't separate this out from its political/philosophical context because – again obviously – the music was a response to events. 'Anarchy' was a racket that raged against fraudulence – foul untruths and complacency in the music industry. Paul Weller was belting out frustrations and capturing the times as we horny, angry young people saw them. Gang of Four were more laser-like, more articulate around politics. But this was a *reaction*. No racism, no North-South divide, no privilege protecting itself – no punk.

Thatcher became leader of the Tories in 1975. I understand that many people view her as heroic but I don't. In any event it would seem unarguable that she was a divisive figure and a catalyst for protest around economic priorities and issues of race, class and community. As I write now there is a sense that Thatcher's view of (say) Apartheid South Africa might be acceptable or even morally sustainable; that equality doesn't matter anymore, somehow isn't real. People of Colour are being broadly and openly demonized by a section of society emboldened by prejudiced political actors and media.

In the UK this is of course the rise of Reform and the fag-end of Conservatism, kept afloat by bigoted press-barons or billionaire technocrats. A brutal and apparently 'populist' agenda built almost entirely around fear and hatred of outsiders. Immigrants. Scroungers. Boat People or Small Boats People. A single, unifying, blunt instrument of policy, utterly predicated on prejudice. In the States it gets scarier still.

It gives me no pleasure to place this in a book about the power and yesss the joy of music. But when the President of the USA is pedaling open vileness and the leader of Reform is openly following his 'strategies' on race and on wokeness *and they are gathering support,* where else do I go but to that which opposes? For civility and to protest for goodness and decency, we go back into art and resistance: largely because our progressive politicians are failing us. But that really is a story for another day.

Trump and Musk are evil and their media superstructure is an extravagant corruption. We see them but many do not; they are sucked into the vortex, enabled by pliant powerhouses and universal systems of messaging that flood filth and vacuity into our heads. These monsters have bought democracy and we need to rage.

I can confirm that rage isn't just a young person's prerogative. But look at what angry or motivated young people can do! And maybe look at *the scope* for influencing. Is there a chink in the armour, here? Could the wit and the brilliance and the increasing presence of snappy wee choons be used positively and even subversively and against the goons? I think it's possible.

Look how GIANT some of the current crop of stars are. (I'm not saying I like them, or they are models of consciousness – of course the majority of HUGE STARS are HUGE STARS because they have at some level conciliated – but is there not hope around this?) More Beyoncé-at-the-Superbowl moments are not only possible, they are likely. More high-profile artists are likely to come out against the effective White Supremacism and the crushing vindictiveness and ignorance of the Trump regime. Possibly more importantly, that whole web of punky, 'street-level' opposition could, as they say, 'go viral'. The very inter-connectedness that facilitated Trump 2 could be turned against him.

I'm no techie but even without the support of fascistically-inclined technocrats, it feels like a Youth Explosion could take hold. Even if punk band equivalents didn't turn up on every corner, calling or bawling-out the dumbos. Don't get me wrong, I'd love to see and hear *actual music*, actual radically-inclined bands pushing back against racism and intolerance, but we may not need that massive volume of activity to arise, simply and perhaps ironically because of the reach of our devices. Despite Musk and co's appalling algorithms, or outside of them, we can Fight The Power. Young people have the knowledge: they're savvy. Even if things go full-on fascist – sadly this is not unthinkable, as I write – musical messaging can penetrate or even swamp the ether. This gives me hope.

What I'm getting at is I can't think of a more vital time for music (& young people) to discover or re-discover their conscience & their *agency*.

NINETEEN – GO ON, THEN. SOME DESERT ISLAND DISCS. FOR PURELY EDUCATIONAL REASONS.

The time is ripe again for some major action. If I could divest myself of the urgency and the perennial fury around this I might say 'fascinatingly so'. But let's leave the analysis to the historians. I'm dead mad and so should you be.

Many of the ingredients have been re-boiled: chiefly that old chestnut prejudice. I get the current trend for 'hearing real people's real concerns about immigration' (for example) but I am also clear that often that is a feeble and even cynical swerve from the legitimate course of action: namely to call out racism. Yes of course this has to be done *in tandem* with processes which manifestly alleviate poverty and discontent. But take no backward steps around the conviction that racism and othering are wrong. Build societies that are better, not whiter.

This is an urgent time again. Could be the imperatives are bigger and more dangerous than at the time of Punk 1. Exhibit A? The blistering campaigning activity by

KNEECAP, around Gaza, focuses the need on **the issue of our times** *and* calls-out the interconnectedness of wider political evils.

Plainly Trump is as culpable as Netanyahu in enabling the genocide against the Palestinians. It's not just in this sense that Punk 2 may need to be more about the US than the UK – although almost wherever you look there are challenges to democracy, integration and hope.

*

Not quite sure where rights land, exactly, in terms of titles and quotes and stuff. (Believe you can't copyright a title but less sure about what else you can pinch: consequently have abstained from sticking in here some of the words that *really have* carried me through. *Would have loved to have done that!*). Am hoping that slapping down a few major choons or moments will be seen for what it is – a kind of tribute – more than an act of pilferation.

We all do this D. I. D thing, don't we? Dunno yet if I'll be keeping it to eight. Will try to be short and sweet – and 'relevant'.

You need to be aware of these:

THE SEX PISTOLS: ANARCHY / PRETTY VACANT / HOLIDAYS. (Oh shit. I can't keep this to eight). Arguable about whether it started here but blimey – where else? These are of course central icons, whatever you may think of Rotten and McLaren, and remain, rather extraordinarily, great noises. They have attitude that will not be mollified. They are a cutting edge. In a way it *did* become a whole lot harder to be mindlessly glib or shamelessly commercially-focused after these moments: although admittedly plenty managed it, bless 'em.

POPTONES / FLOWERS OF ROMANCE / RISE are phase two, Lydon. So PUBLIC IMAGE LIMITED, aka Pil. Sparser and further away from wall-of-sound punk, the first two with a stirring, unsettling level of challenge. (It's rarely acknowledged how goddam *intelligent* and *ambitious* these records are). Music and imagery make 'Pop Tones' the peak of something – abstraction? Reflection? Provocation? It's a worldie for its unzipping of the violent blandness of the universe. 'Rise' is comparatively easy-listening. But fabulous rolling riff.

THE BUZZCOCKS: BOREDOM / EVER FALLEN are that wonderful, almost-cheesy-but-*knowing* end of the power-pop market. Buzzcocks as fabulous bees, with their worker-drone droning. Modest but irresistibly triumphant; without, of course, the triumphalism. Certainly not threatening: so just that sense of guitar-music being brought up-to-date. Ironic but also very playful. Street thrash for street trash like us. Some of their singles were a kind of perfection.

TALKING HEADS: LIFE DURING WARTIME / PSYCHOKILLER bring us into tetchy artsy-land. So departing: getting smart. Some theatre in there... and tremendous lyrics. Fast choppy guitar and levels of intelligence and irony to spare. Tremendously groovy;

sinuous and contemporary in a way that felt closer to us Brits than many US bands did. Left-field mainstream, I suppose, but post-punk. 'Fear Of Music' is flawlessly executed.

GANG OF FOUR: DAMAGED GOODS E.P. and actually 'ENTERTAINMENT'. Andy Gill's guitar encapsulated something really thrilling about the subversive and urgent nature of new wave music. And the words were a stunning counterpoint to all that free-but-edgy rhythm-making. Brainy, political stuff, strangely(?) dispassionately(?) delivered. These guys had an essence that was indeed rare – cerebral and white-funktastic. They brought their manifesto to the front. They were 'dour' and magbloodynificent.

THE SLITS: TYPICAL GIRLS / CUT. Colourful dub-punk… or something. Again smacking of Brains In Action – so post pogoing or gobbing – but essentially another great band who sought to unzip the easy normalcies of The Industry. Feminist *and* fun. Kinda druggy but check out the sharpness in 'Typical Girls'. Strikingly original production, for which Denis Bovell must get a note in passing. Important that punk had a) strong, visible women and b) something that registered as multi-cultural.

ELVIS COSTELLO: RADIO RADIO / NEW LACE SLEEVES / shedloads of brilliance. A huge influence. Deliberately uncool; extravagantly articulate. Angry as hell but roving with serene and controlled confidence across the songwriting universe, smashing it wherever he went. 'Radio Radio' is faaar too bright to shine solely as a popsong. 'New Lace Sleeves' is a staggering, deceptive protest. Unthinkable without punk, but transcended into a zillion genres out of creative need and *unreal* and unreally prolific songwriting. Seven arguably unsurpassable consecutive albums in the new wave era. Mind-blowing.

101-ers/CLASH: KEYS TO YOUR HEART / WHITE MAN / WORKING FOR THE CLAMPDOWN. 'Keys' remains a fave – though some of this inevitably 'about sentiment'. The low-fi strummability and the Strummer vocal are just ace. Then Big Clash Noises. Power chords. 'White Man' spilling out of reggae; 'Clampdown' driving hard but spacey. The anger and subversion we had to have. Had to watch our steps, us Grimsby Lads, at Sheffield Top Rank but wow.

THE JAM: IN THE CITY / MR CLEAN / WHEN YOU'RE YOUNG. I've listened again, during the writing of this book and it's made me feel closer to Weller. (And I absolutely loved The Jam, from the outset!) Think maybe I'd lost a little of that sense of how furious and yes radical some of the material was – or how furiously Weller delivered it. 'Mr Clean' is full of a whole lot of contempt for the vacuousness and conciliation of Everyday Life. It doesn't sound like a punk record – nothing after the first year or so did. But it both fired us angry-young-fekkers up and *represented us*. I've noted 'When You're Young' here for its fabulous energy and rousing guitar but truth be told, as per several other key bands from the era, I could've picked out almost any one of a series of truly mighty singles.

MAGAZINE: SONG FROM UNDER THE FLOORBOARDS. Not as hooky and infectious as 'Shot By Both Sides', but this remains etched into my heart/soul/ whatever it is we have for our Deep Shit. It's the answer to anyone who says popular music is dumb or has no integrity. It's the answer to anyone who thinks new wave was a meaningless racket. It's staggering and beautiful and profound and we may have no right to expect rock and roll could be this wonderful, this far-reaching. But this is. I may yet get drunk and go to a tattoo parlour. I may never stop quoting the lyrics to myself or to family gatherings. Cheers, Howard. This has mattered.

JOY DIVISION: TRANSMISSION / ISOLATION / ATMOSPHERE. All have to be in here, despite further departures from punk. The first is one of the greatest singles ever recorded. The second is an astonishing, rich diversion and the third is like some mountain-peak for beautiful, profound, aesthetic, soulful music. There is much sadness around Joy Division but maaan there is elation and exultation, too. They coloured the depths. They found us. They understood.

THE SPECIALS: IT DOESN'T MAKE IT ALRIGHT / GANGSTERS / GHOST TOWN – etc. Specials covered all the bases and god-knows-how but they got to all of them brilliantly. Wit; fun; fury; youth; politics; dancing. Shit nightclubs and dangerous streets. Racist wankers and concrete jungles. Proper fusion of love, ideas, comradeship, influence.

Often they made it sound simple – witness 'It Doesn't Make It'. Sometimes, as in 'Ghost Town'/'Gangsters',

things were deliciously rich and musically ambitious –
Dammers could do that thing. But they felt close to us.
Kindof ordinary. Kindof at our level. Facing the stuff we
faced; writing and singing about our experience and our
time. They came out of punk and they took us somewhere
else, whilst keeping that precious conscience, whilst being
rooted in the real. I don't idolize people (I don't think):
but I miss Terry Hall.

Outliers? Blimey – much better not to think. Fall, ATV,
Television. How far we drifting? R.E.M and B52s. 'Levi
Stubb's Tears' perhaps strangely… but what a song!
Plenty of Bunnymen choons and 'Poor Old Soul' and
'Blueboy' from the fabulous Orange Juice. These I'd
have to consider, before jumping into the dhow. But
onwards, beating, towards the end.

TWENTY – PALATE-CLEANSER.

Where are we, with tribute bands? Not sure I'd ever seen one until...

Went to see a Johnny Cash tribute band on a Friday night in Milford Haven. February 2025. The man sits somewhere on the outside-edge of my listening but ENTERTAINMENT beckoned – remember that? – and female company was in the mix, so I went. It was a howling gale: that lovely clanging and ringing of masts and rigs was broiling up from the harbour, starlike but not bible-black. Torch Theatre was bright and welcoming and rammed. There was that authentic and unmistakable buzz, pre- a live event.

I confess I had genned-up, not wanting to be the only non-ardent fan in the building, and became increasingly interested in the life-story that emerged. Some of the songs I knew: we all do.

Johnny died in 2003. He was a strange mix: speed addict, on and off, over many years. Baptist and associate of Billy Graham. Serial adulterer. Accidental arsonist – having set fire to half of California. Specialist jail performer and occasional prisoner himself, for minor misdemeanours: (incarcerated several times, just for the one night). **Voice for the Oppressed** *– in* *particular Native Americans. 'Undertaker' and 'Man in Black'. One of the biggest-selling recording artists of all time.*

In the Sixties, Cash boldly championed American Indian rights. He raged at the music industry, posting a letter in Billboard magazine accusing the business of cowardice around the historical fact. 'Bitter Tears: Ballads of the American Indian', from 1964, redressed the imbalance by focussing entirely on violence against and theft of land and dignity. It was and remains an extraordinary statement. 'The Ballad of Ira Hayes' stands out as a tremendous, pictorial and poignant icon of protest, telling the story of a staged flag-raising at Iwo Jima. (Ira was one of six US soldiers involved... and a Native American).

Scoot forward to our Pembrokeshire winter. 'Cash' himself (himself) is impersonating and not. Handsome, dark; authentic-looking quiff. His own man in a confident and engaging way. Outstanding, seasoned musicians are on stand-up bass and guitar. There's a teenager on drums (or so it seems) and a backing-singer who brings just the right amount of knees-up energy and commitment.

In short they were what we Taffs call 'class'. It was a stonking night out, with half of Milford dancing in the aisles in that proper-lovely, undemonstrative, (OK intoxicated) but lost-in-music kindofaway that speaks much more of real, natural connections – musical and social – than of performative nights out. Yes there was some talk of Cash's life and conscience but this was entertainment central. Two sets banged-out with charm, professionalism and an infectious humour that reminded those of us who needed it that not everything needs to be seeking to change the world. Or maybe better still, even stuff that makes you grin can change the world.

JC was a deeply flawed man, loved and respected not just for that distinctive voice and singular image. He brought messages – brought strong medicine.

I missed a good deal of that contribution first time around and I'm unconcerned that our shindig in Milford may have offered more fun than political awakening. The strength of the fayre – the 'belters'; the 'artists' – was intoxicating and invigorating enough. I stepped out into the gale again inwardly smiling and possibly even humming; having been nudged back towards some genuinely deep and evocative songwriting. People were swaying, cwtching-up and lighting ciggies. Beat that.

TWENTY-ONE – 'CONCLUSIONS'.

Clearly and for obvious reasons, everybody holds tight to the music of their teens. I get that. It's just natural. It's gonna feel special. But this is 1976/7/8/9. It feels like the streets are on fire and sometimes they are. There are Thatcherian (was that ever even a word?) or what we might nowadays term Trumpian levels of divisiveness and even hatred in the political ether. There's Johnny Rotten and Joe Strummer and Paul Weller... and that new sound a-rumbling.

(In my humble view) around about NOW is the greatest time in the history of popular music. For the energy and the *meaning* – however flawed or obscured by inadequate explication, however feebly received by the pogoing masses. Something was *really happening*. Throw in being a tumultuously hormonal young fella with a powerful sense that things aren't right or fair; plus shock and existential confusion over a family tragedy or two. Why wouldn't you attach, pretty directly and permanently, to the soundtrack of these life-changing moments?

The Scene *was* mad, rich and diverse, powered by an energy that still feels special. The industries of fashion and rock and roll did of course look to package and commodify and there were loads of fakers – there always are, right? But Westwood and McLaren (for example) were part of the creative force *as well as* the commercial exploitation or exercise. Bands seemed to understand something about the need to re-connect to ordinary lives. It felt more possible that band members might be ordinary people. Perhaps most satisfyingly – yes; so good I'm saying it twice – the advent of Independent Record Labels, or more exactly their *proliferation*, made the theoretical practical. The barriers had been trampled.

Stiff Records, Rough Trade and Fast Records made good on the punky promise that all of us could have a crack at this: that virtuosity and commercial focus were not prerequisites. Real People could make records.

This independence, this *spirit* bred or fed into a kind of anti-cool which you can probably still feel, bristling between these pages. Or'nary Herberts could get up and do stuff. Me; you; Fergal Sharkey; Mark E Smith. They could record it, too, and access to new technologies would only increase, thereby (theoretically at least) multiplying the opportunities. New and often more personal or political messages could be sent out from voices previously unheard.

This was the Great De-mystification. The offering. You no longer had to be 'musical', or ambitious, or on a contract with a major. Get playing.

*

The possibilities were sharp and they were rich. I loved something about Alternative Television's 'How Much Longer', which provided a fabulous, 'niche', committed, critical response to punk fashion. Former journo Mark Perry bawled out stuff about not knowing naffink and not caring. It was quintessentially DIY and defiantly Essex (or similar). Meanwhile New Yoik's Television were expanding the known (pre-indie) universe with the iconic 'Marquee Moon', which re-set the whole of rock by drawing out its dumb machismo. They chimed with intelligence and no little artistry, but beautifully and surgically removed the testosterone. It was all guitars and wow – no posing.

The New Populist Energy thing – I say again, *in a good way* – was interpreted and transformed all over the shop. Stiff Little Fingers (who were probably pret-ty authentically punk) banged out resonating power chords and sounded like their place. Blondie went HUGE, losing the rawness of 'Rip Her To Shreds' and finding chart-friendly but listenable pop – 'Denis, Denis'/'I am always Touched' – before showcasing (or appropriating) rap. The Skids, initially fronted by a prominent male model, were largely faking it but had an engagingly raw guitar sound and were electrifying live. Boomtown Rats were absolutely faking it – as was Billy Idol, as were plenty others – but their new wave-lite, being unthreateningly radio-friendly, loomed large. Some of The Giants – Bowie, Springsteen? – were listening in and definitely re-energised.

Ver-ry familiar with those 'it started in New Yoik or somewhere else states-side' arguments but experience makes that irrelevant. The Surge that *gathered us* was tectonically-charged by Pistols, Clash, Jam (and yeh) McLaren and Westwood – so London calling – but the likes of Fall, ATV, Buzzcocks and Gang of Four, amongst many others, were essential to that mad ride. How could that not feel not just local but visceral? *In* the body; *of* our place?

Gonna sound like some Dumb Californian if I say punk was a *cause* more than a sonic experience – although it was often definitively the latter. It got bastardised, corrupted, used from the outset but if you haven't grasped that Lydon's twin cries for anarchy *and* that he did you no wrong *were both about not just change but change of moral compass*, then you haven't received the message. The Bizz is shite; phoney, pacifying, 'organized' everyday life is shite and we need to make it better, by being real. By telling honest, relevant stories and screaming from the rooftops or the stage-front that we don't need to be musicians to perform. We all have value and we have the right and the power to be heard. Death to indulgence and schmaltz; death to anaesthetic 'pop' and courting posterity. Gimme three chords and tell me about your life!

*

Could be there are almost no great punk bands because a) they were swallowed into the puppetry and pomp of The Bizz or b) they were too dumb, flawed or drug-influenced to make a sustained case. Could be only a few individuals *really understood* the political-philosophical imperative towards honesty and cutting truths, in any case. Where are the convincing spokespeople? Even Lydon and Strummer were patently imperfect advocates, despite being the two great voices on vinyl.

Understand that there's a case that it's only the records that count, not some manifesto preached to John Peel, Terry Wogan, Chris Tarrant. The vinyl is the validation and the seminal notch in history but it's always frustrated me that so few of those involved have articulated the specialness of punk and that unsurpassable post-punk wave, either at or after the time. When it's kinda simple. Values were re-set; the power of honest, unpretentious art was re-stated; truth and relevance *mattered*; access was wide.

Some made a punk record or two by accident or aligned with the vibe but lacked the intention or commitment towards holding the universe to account. Others liked the theatre of the whole thing – Siouxsie? – so went pretty promptly from punk icon to goth art-school-rocker. (Banshees made a thrilling racket but departed early-doors. Even The Scream, original and bright as it was, felt closer to conciliation than radicalised verve).

The p-word (or at least The P Experience) was all about immediacy, urgency, spittle; about kinds of revolution in the now, because of the now. In our case that meant Thatcher, injustice and anger. The North-South divide. Racism. Homophobia – later enshrined in the law in the infamous Section 28 – but a part of the Thatcherite vocab well before HIV struck in 1981. Shameless boom for some, bust for many. We can be entirely specific that

Thatcherism was a signal factor in the emergence of a furious counter-culture.[64]

But back to timelines and longevity. The relative absence of compelling, let alone godlike Purveyors-of-the-New-Truth and/or the assimilation or dilution of the punk ethos into and across established stars and (the general, succeeding) New Wave may have contributed to the limited span of the phenomenon. However, because of the glorious monsters and fabulous, sweet-but-true singles spawned directly from its raging heart, undeniable traces flooded out and on. They remain with us, thank god.

Costello was of the era and his contribution to both music generally and the particular niche for stories-with-integrity may be matchless, over the last fifty years. He is an honorary punk and one of the more obvious examples of how or why you can't *just* write protest songs; or if you *did* they'd inevitably morph towards sophistication and 'maturity' – towards grown-up music.

Early Elvis was very much a persona. But not only did he look kinda right he knocked out some utterly brilliant protest songs – 'Radio, Radio' and the poppier, ironically more radio-friendly 'Oliver's Army' – almost shockingly promptly. However, the Costello oeuvre

---

[64] It wasn't 'til I looked harder at this that I twigged that Thatcher became Tory Party leader in *1975*. It may have taken four more years before she ascended... but something in the ether had changed. Punk was one of *our responses*.

included romantic ('Alison') and observational or relationship-oriented gems ('The Angels Wanna Wear My) Red Shoes') from the first album. Of course it did: the bloke had things to say.

Some make the argument that EC's simply written too many songs – Wikipedia cites 33 studio albums, 6 live albums, 17 compilation albums, 6 tribute albums, 2 Eps, 62 singles and 4 box sets. (A-and breathe). There may be something to this but if nothing else it reminds us that the scope of material to sustain any career has to be rich and wide. (So not possible to just live off anger).

*

Being the touchstones of integrity, purpose and inspiration we needed (and some of them set out to be) was and is quite the challenge. Some of our other early anti-heroes inevitably 'moved on' musically, shortening the lifespan of punk – though not necessarily its influence.

Weller was engagingly, often excitingly spiky early doors – the first Jam album was thrashtastic and low-fi and (s)punky. It had the energy of the moment. Later he split what was probably the best band in the world to write film music and stuff with the Style Council, before transitioning again into the occasionally edgy Establishment Geezer he is now. Few doubt his integrity, but the liberal use of orchestras and orchestration in his more recent career feels a long way from 'When You're Young' and is less appealing to me.

The boy Rotten had real genius as well as daft, spiteful prejudice. Mark E Smith was never a punk but he brought that fearless 'ordinary' voice and the angularity, the un-compromise that made a zillion garage bands possible. Siouxsie, Poly Styrene then Slits and Raincoats piled in to de-cock the new rock.

After 'Anarchy' and 'White Riot' and 'In The City', to be credible, you had to write about something. Cut the frills and the solos. Tell us what fires you up... or at least stop seeking adoration. Tell us a meaningful story. Do it now.

TWENTY-TWO – MOPPING-UP.

Power chords are actual things... but typically I've been thinking of them in an abstracted way, to suit my evil porpoises. They are fifths, or they are comprised of a root note plus a fifth; or they are dyads; or they are subject to characteristic frequencies or modulations or other stuff that makes your head hurt. Mainly, they are punky or heavy versions of chords lending themselves to distortion and impact, in a choon.

They are often easy to play, coz no third (so can't be either major or minor, strictly-speaking). But yeh; your head can hurt trying to understand or relate this accurately. This is not my intention. *Generally* the use of a phrase to suggest something of mood or feel is closer to my intention, and it's therefore medium-satisfying to see the fekker alighting on the front page of this book.

One of the great legacies of punk is of course the whole idea that you don't have to be 'good' in the great tradition. In fact why would you want to be, when by the mid-late seventies much of contemporary music was either 'competent' and commercial-but-saccharoidal shite or the posturings of supergroups? What was so great about air-head-slick pop or masturbatory indulgence? Punk was necessary to flush out revelatory truths about energy and honesty and commitment, to gob hard at all those wanky wafts at the ethereal. Bollocks to chasing posterity: the new wave spoke urgently to the now, storming the gates (even storming the charts, god forbid!) with *real ideas.*

Suddenly, music need not infer nor be predicated upon musicality – which probably relies on talent, which often relies upon privilege. That's probably lesson 2 of punk. (Lesson 1 was 'you can do this wiv freee chords!') Punk demanded that songs be *about something,* as opposed to being about posing or gathering moolah.

John Lydon wasn't a singer; neither was Ian Curtis. They were the Different Voices we needed – they were reactions to the black hole, the vacancy that was the entertainment industry. *They were in opposition.*

Thrillingly, in this new era, you didn't need to sing to be a singer: but you probably had to say something. The days of Robert Plant wailing about baby(s) were (if not exactly numbered) at least under threat. Cock rock wasn't good enough; twiddly solos weren't good enough; musicality itself wasn't enough. In this context we were all in wivva chance. That was the whole point.

I am not immune to the argument that Bowie and Bolan are amongst those who paved the way towards punk. (If you listen to 'Suffragette City' and 'Twentieth Century Boy' – both I believe from 1973 – the snarl and grind of the guitar sound may well be anticipating new wave). And in any case it feels likely or 'natural' that obscure, tangential or unknowable influences seeped in to the consciousness of the era – so go find or recover your own.

For me, Bowie, despite the grand and some would say subversive visuals, was essentially conservative – essentially in concert with the industry. (I know many would disagree). He felt, to us punky lads, like an admittedly colourful, occasionally brilliant compartment of the train we wanted to wreck. The imagery was often literally fantastic but the songs were distractions... and *about what*, exactly? Famously, he went around the place like he was David bloody Bowie. We didn't want to escape with him, or back into the hallucinogenic faerie-land with Bolan. Thatcher and fury at the Big Beast of Greed loomed too large. There were skin'eads and bankers and racist cops; issues we had to take on.

Despite many of us loving 'Hunky Dory', I guess we associated this cracked actor-geezer with the whole industry of fauxness and broader commercial *theatre*; with the mainstays of giant record companies and giant shows. So despite acknowledging a kind of greatness (in terms of his *contribution*), we punkettes did, justifiably, even now I think, cast him off alongside your Roxy Musics and your Pink Floyds. We did have that austerity-thing going on. We did judge. Brutally.

Maybe some of this was or is about the difference between LSD/hallucinogens and coke and amphetamines? Maybe we had a focus that they didn't? Punk raged against the false, the arty, the facile – the indulgent. It bawled its messages, angrily and urgently, because it *actually wanted* change.

From Lydon's coruscating, flawed-but-electrifying moral fury ('I did you no wrong!') to Costello's intelligent, extravagant gift of Songs With Meaning, this, the period of my youthful/manful turning was a rich time. We were on fire with the knowledge that music had invented a new integrity and purpose. We knew it was special: it underpinned us. We took no prisoners in terms of judging who was really with us and who smacked of appeasement or worse.

*

The longer and further I have gotten into this book, the more obviously it has loomed that the State of the Universe prods us closer to another time when young oiks might need to be bawling their raging hearts out.

This has been a Brit-centric missive but having only recently escaped from the worst and most obviously corrupt series of governments of my entire lifetime – Tory governments, to be clear – only to feel the heavy shadow of the Trump/Musk axis looming over all of us, the climate has shifted. We Brits or English-speaking Europeans feel more acutely exposed to North American issues, perhaps because The Internet, and certainly because our US-based socials are swamping us by design. The shitstorm that Bannon boasted about *has captured us, too.*

I'm a little fascinated by this idea that the need for resistance feels so huge (to me/to us?) despite the geography having shifted a few thousand miles west.

It's true I am lower-level-furious about Starmer's vacuity and Reeve's obsession with growth but that anger isn't at punk-revolution pitch – not quite.[65] So this book, this fug of a hypothesis may be moving towards a proxy protest... which gets us into all kinds of bother about legitimacy and truth. We may in fact be flopping into a full-on irony-fest, given our previous and superior prejudices about the good folks of the US. Brits may now be in a right carry-on, of the 'Vicariously Angry On Behalf Of You Yanks' variety. Coz you need a reaction most, yes?

It's a mess and it may be ver-ry scary. But I have some hope that voices of protest will and are once more rising up, reaching for the music in all of our souls. Brothers, sisters, however you identify; we need you.

---

[65] Update: as of May 2025... and Gaza ongoing and Labour now openly demonizing immigrants, the situation may be evolving.

AFTERWORDS.

This may be the last book I write. Am not clear on this, but it's possible. It may be an Ode to Music in the same way that 'Beautiful Games' is an Ode to Sport, or Sports Development. 'The Dots Will Not Be Joined' is both joined at the hip and a sort of deliberately wild and wide-ranging provocation: my statement against linearity and the dumbness of much of our thinking. I like these books. They've been a mad indulgence in financial terms but... honestly? I've gone the Independent Record Label route and made up my own lingo. How big a factor do you think Commercial Viability has been in all of this?

I like the obvious own-goals, the lean into bad writing and the all-round daft immaturity. Take it as seriously as you like. This is personal but not. There's lots of me in here because that seems like a direct (and therefore hopefully honest) route into truths I know about. Clearly I'm an outlier in the sense of being 'in my own voice'. Yup, for better or worse.

I have no fear of being judged on any level but that of veracity. By that I mean the truth in the relating of the stories: the *intention*. This has not been about me being bright or brilliant at stuff; I'm plainly not. There are no incredi-achievements in these books – not by me.[66] But there is a significant dollop of love, wonder and respect splattered across these pages. Plus there are challenges, across the wild range of my experience and aspiration. I hope I haven't joined too many dots.

*

Almost certainly swore I wouldn't do this but...

You wake up with Colin Moulding. Boodadumm/ bopdedoodadumm/bopdedoodadum. And "the first time a saw you standing at the warr-der-ahur". ('Statue of Liberty'). And you think 'Jesus. XTC!!' And you think about how much you loved them, through those first two albums. Seeing them live at some college gig: spectacular, crisp, funny. Knowing they're not punk but bringing that zing and wit and power. Andy Partridge hiding behind that flimsy veil of Twisted Englishness... but still being lovely, cos he can't bloody help it. XTC being *absolutely brilliant*, from keyboards on up. A sort of Temporary Beauty in my life – like the mighty Graham Parker was. But also here, now, today. Because, like your faves – the ones I stupidly forgot to insert here – they did some wonderful, entertaining, heavy-lifting stuff.

*

And the hand? Not great. Make the assumption that these are the last words on the last day, before I park this baby with the publishers.

---

[66] It's not just Elvis Costello that I failed to be – lols.

It's Mon 7th July 2025. Nowhere near making a fist so chords aren't really happening. Will keep at it but for the first time yesterday I did wonder about switching to bass. That feels *possible*.

"A-one two-three-four"...